A GUIDE TO MODERNISM IN METRO-LAND

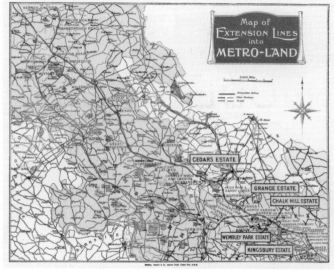

Chronicle/Alamy Stock Photo

A GUIDE TO MODERNISM IN METRO-LAND

Joshua Abbott

unbound

First published in 2020

Unbound
Level 1, Devonshire House, One Mayfair Place, London W1J 8AJ
www.unbound.com

Maps by Martin Lubikowski, ML Design, London
Contains OS data © Crown copyright and
database right (2019)

Text Design by Patty Rennie

A CIP record for this book is available from the British Library

ISBN 978-1-78352-856-1 (paperback)
ISBN 978-1-78352-857-8 (ebook)

Printed in Slovenia by DZS Grafik

9 8 7 6 5 4 3 2

Contents

Metro-Land and Modernism

The idea of Metro-Land has been around for just over one hundred years now. In 1915 an employee of the Metropolitan Railway, James Garland, came up with the concept of Metro-Land to help sell some of the excess land the Met had acquired in extending its railways out from the capital into the fields of Middlesex. The expansion of the Metropolitan Railway was driven by the company's general manager, Robert Selbie, who wanted an extension to link the capital to villages such as Wembley, Harrow, Pinner and Ruislip, and towns like Amersham and Aylesbury. The surplus land was handed over to a newly formed company, the Metropolitan Railway Country Estates Limited [MRCE], which drew up plans to create commuter suburbs at some of the villages along the new railway. The first estates were built at Neasden [Kingsbury Garden Village], Wembley [Wembley Garden Suburb], Pinner [Cecil Park and the Grange Estate] and Rickmansworth [the Cedars Estate]. These new garden villages were largely fashioned in the arts and crafts style, created by architects such as Oliver Hill who designed some of Wembley Garden Village.

The idea of Metro-Land, echoed by the tiled cottages of the garden villages, was to create a rural idyll for the commuter to escape to [via the Metropolitan Railway] after a day in the city. Posters show houses surrounded by gardens and parks where the harassed white collar worker could enjoy his free time and live in harmony with nature [at least until Monday morning]. Metro-Land didn't just have the MCRE to publicise it, but also its own poet laureate. John Betjeman hymned Metro-Land praises in verses such as 'Harrow-on-the-Hill' and 'Middlesex', where the poet talked of obscure places like Perivale, Wealdstone and Ruislip Gardens. Later his *Metro-Land* documentary, broadcast in 1973, would become a television classic.

The question *what is Metro-Land?* is easier to define than *where is Metro-Land?* As the MRCE-produced *Metro-Land* guide famously said, it is 'a country with elastic borders that each visitor can draw for himself as Stevenson drew his map of Treasure Island', an idea rather than a geographical marking. However, we can shade the map in a little. Taking the aforementioned villages, moving out in a line north-west from Baker Street, we can see Metro-Land moving out of the capital from Neasden, taking in Wembley, Harrow, Ruislip, Pinner and then on to Amersham. Of course its influence didn't stick to this tidy trajectory, extending right around suburban London, taking in such places as Enfield, Barnet, Watford, Greenford, Ealing, Hillingdon, Hayes and the spreading ribbon developments of the capital.

Being influenced by the garden suburb movement and due to its innate Englishness, the default architectural style of Metro-Land was nostalgic, a mixture of mock Tudor and Elizabethan nicknamed Tudorbethan [a phrase coined by Betjeman. This hybrid style mixed traditional designs on the exterior, and the comforts of modernity such as electricity and indoor plumbing inside. However, outbreaks of modernism did occur in this realm of wistfulness. Charles Holden's London Underground stations are the most prominent example. His functional 'Sudbury Box' design first appeared at Sudbury Town in 1931, and its pared-down brick and glass minimalism set a template for stations throughout suburbia. Another widespread but lesser-known example of the modernism being built in Metro-Land are the schools of Curtis and Burchett for Middlesex County Council. The duo designed and built a swathe of schools throughout the county, often with their signature Willem Dudok-influenced central staircase tower. The pair also built other municipal facilities such as clinics, libraries, courthouses and police stations.

There was also room among the mock timber for the white-walled, flat-roofed house. The short-lived but highly influential partnership of Welch, Cachemaille-Day and Lander built a large number of deco-influenced 'suntrap' houses throughout the 1930s, as well as more robust-looking brick dwellings in Hendon and on the Hanger Hill estate in Ealing. The darlings of the International Style in Britain were the partnership of Connell, Ward and Lucas. Their signature house 'High and Over' nestles in the green hills of Amersham on the Metropolitan Line, designed in a Y plan for Professor Bernard Ashmole. Perhaps even more cutting edge was their plan for a whole estate in Ruislip, of which only three houses were completed, 97, 99 and 101 Park Avenue. The art deco cinema was also in its golden age during the rise of Metro-Land, and many great examples still exist such as the Rayners Lane Grosvenor by local architect F. E. Bromige.

Much has changed in Metro-Land in the post-war period. Just as Metro-Land had itself swallowed up tiny villages, the ever-growing metropolis submerged the Arcadian ideal sold in those posters from the MCRE. Now the former villages and garden suburbs of Wembley, Pinner and Harrow have become part of the endless exterior sprawl of London, losing some of their unique character. And of course the growth of modernism in Metro-Land didn't stop, but became part of the state-sanctioned post-war redevelopment. The harsher brutalist-style buildings of the fifties, sixties and seventies did not proliferate in the suburbs as much as in Central and East London, but there are some good examples of buildings by Ernő Goldfinger, Owen Luder and the Smithsons in this area. Borough councils emboldened by the 1965 reorganisation went on a building spree, creating homes, hospitals and libraries for their growing populations. Much of this municipal building followed the trends and ideas of post-war architecture, but some innovative architecture departments like those at Hillingdon or Haringey broke with the high-rise orthodoxy and designed buildings on a smaller, more intimate scale.

As redevelopment rumbles ever onward, many monuments to modernism in Metro-Land are disappearing. Just in the last few years a number of buildings have been demolished, such as the Palace of Industry at Wembley and the Electricity Showrooms in Willesden. That of course is the impetus behind this book, to document these wonderful and half-forgotten buildings before they disappear through accident or design, and to allow the twenty-first century visitor to Metro-Land to create their own modernist county with elastic borders.

Author's Note

This section is intended for me to explain the various choices I have made in creating the guide: the area covered, the buildings included and the arrangement of the guide. All of these choices will no doubt elicit questions, and hopefully the following will go some way to answering them

As mentioned in 'Metro-Land and Modernism', Metro-Land is of course an idea rather than a place, and different people will sketch different borders for this imaginary county. For this guide I have decided to draw the borders using the county of Middlesex between 1930 and its abolition in 1965. This area includes the 'original' Metro-Land (areas like Wembley, Harrow and Pinner) as well as what I think of as 'greater' Metro-Land (Barnet, Hounslow, Richmond, etc.). It also allows the guide to be neatly divided into the London boroughs that replaced Middlesex in 1965. Of course, Metro-Land's elastic borders did stretch into Hertfordshire and Buckinghamshire, so I have included the parts of those counties I feel were affected by the Metropolitan Railway's expansion in the early twentieth century.

I have been exploring the modernist buildings of Metro-Land since 2011, when I began photographing them as part of a university photography project; later on it became a website. I wanted to choose a selection of these for the guide, to show the reader what I thought was most worth seeking out in each area. This selection consists of well-known buildings that are the best examples of modernism from their time (such as Highpoint), lesser-known buildings that deserve to seen (Kingsley Court) or buildings that help explain how the suburbs grew in the first half of the twentieth century (Sudbury Town tube station). Of course buildings will be left out that readers will feel should have been included, but a guidebook must select some and discard others.

The other two factors in terms of choosing which buildings to feature are chronological and stylistic. There was no 'big bang' moment in terms of modernism arriving in Britain; buildings gradually appeared here and there with modernistic elements from the late nineteenth century, but the 1930s was when this trickle became a stream. The earliest building in the book dates from 1912 and the latest from 1990, eighty years of architectural fashion swinging one way and another. In terms of style, the buildings I have included run a gamut of appearances and intentions, from art deco and the International Style to brutalism and high tech. I have even included a few buildings designed in a quite non-modernist way, such as the remarkable housing designed by Ernest Trobridge in Brent between the wars, not modernist but certainly metro-land.

Lastly, a word on the arrangement of the guide. I have arranged the buildings according to what London borough or county they are in, which seems a straightforward choice. Within each area section I have arranged the buildings in chronological order. This is a less straightforward choice, buildings in guides normally being arranged geographically. I have done this for two reasons. First, this is supposed to be a practical book to use while exploring the suburbs, and I want the reader to plan their own routes rather than follow mine, selecting which buildings *they* want to see. In addition, arranging the buildings chronologically allows the reader to see the way the modernist buildings have changed form and purpose from the start of the twentieth century to its close.

I have given the name of each building as they were originally built, so for example the Empire Pool rather than Wembley Arena. I did this firstly to show the original function of the building, and secondly because the names of buildings are liable to change and so the original name keeps a fixed identity. Also included in the information is the postcode for each building and the nearest tube or rail station to each building. The photographs I have included of the buildings have been taken over the last eight years. This means there may be some discrepancies between the appearance of a building in the book and how it looks when you visit it. Just as with a name, a building's appearance can fluctuate somewhat.

As this is a guide designed to allow people to see the best modernist buildings in the suburbs, I have not included buildings that cannot be viewed from the street. As such, notable designs such as Shrubs Wood in Buckinghamshire by Mendelsohn and Chermayeff are not included. In the same spirit I have not included buildings that are currently in the process of demolition or redevelopment, for instance the Grahame Park Estate in Barnet.

There may be some who will disagree with the choices I have made and explained here, but they were mine to make, and I hope that the selections I have made will help the reader to discover the wonderful variety of modernist buildings in Metro-Land.

'Metro-Land is a country with elastic borders that each visitor can draw for himself, as Stevenson drew his map of Treasure Island'

Metro-Land, 1924

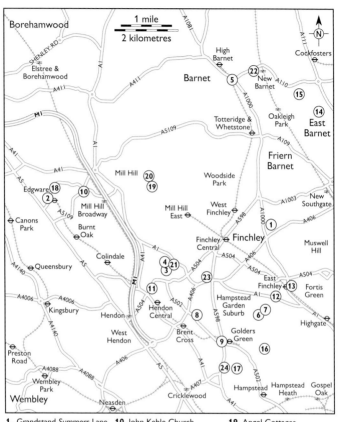

1. Grandstand, Summers Lane
2. Old Rectory Gardens
3. Ashley Lane
4. White House
5. Barnet Odeon
6. 28 Spencer Drive
7. Lytton Close
8. Highfield Court
9. 2 Golders Green Road
10. John Keble Church
11. Hendon Methodist Church
12. Belvedere Court
13. East Finchley Station
14. Brookside Primary
15. Oaklands Infants
16. Spaniards End
17. Beechworth Close
18. Library, Hale Lane
19. Angel Cottages
20. Kingshead House
21. Hendon Hall Court
22. St John's United
    Reformed Church
23. Finchley United Synagogue
24. 83 West Heath Road

BARNET

Barnet is probably the most rural of the northern boroughs, with the countryside appearing just north of High Barnet, and villages such as Totteridge and Monken Hadley maintaining a semi-rural air. Much of the borough is residential, with seemingly endless streets of semi-detached houses spreading out through Hendon and Finchley. The style of most of these houses is overwhelmingly arts and crafts derived, influenced by the Hampstead Garden Suburb homes of Parker and Unwin, in the borough's south-eastern corner. However, Barnet is also home to a number of interesting modernist buildings, mainly residential and largely built in the 1930s. The garden suburb has a number of moderne houses by the likes of Ernst Freud and Welch, Cachemaille-Day and Lander. 'Moderne' is the name usually given to a style somewhere between the curves of Art Deco and the formalism of Modernism, shorn of the extremes of either style. Apartment buildings are well served too, with the stark Highfield Court, Golders Green by A. V. Pilichowski, and the more approachable Belvedere Court, East Finchley by Ernst Freud. In addition to homes, there are smaller works by masters of concrete like Owen Williams and Ernő Goldfinger. Possibly due to its strong Jewish community, Barnet shows the influence of a number of émigré architects from the 1930s, such as Freud.

As for post-war buildings, the home is still king. There are impressive mid-century houses in Hampstead, Mill Hill and Golders Green, although many hide behind tall hedges and impenetrable fences. Northern Barnet was part of Hertfordshire until 1965, and so is home to a few of the pioneering Hertfordshire County Council schools of post 1945, with two good examples in the East Barnet area. Although not to the same standard as other boroughs, the post-1965 Barnet Borough architects' department did produce a few worthwhile projects. The biggest was the Grahame Park housing estate in Colindale, designed in collaboration with the Greater London Council and built between 1969 and 1976. Originally designed in a stark brutalist style, the estate was redesigned in the late 1980s, softening many of its harsher edges. The estate is currently being regenerated by the borough, with new blocks being built and the old buildings being demolished. Libraries was an area Barnet also enjoyed some success in, with modernist-influenced libraries in Finchley, Burnt Oak and Edgware. Unfortunately the current council austerity programme means many of these educational buildings are under threat.

GRANDSTAND, SUMMERS LANE

1930   Grade II

Percival T. Harrison and Owen Williams

 West Finchley N12 0PD

Sports grandstand built for the Finchley Urban District Council, and designed by borough architect Percival T. Harrison with engineering advice from Owen Williams. It is the oldest reinforced concrete cantilevered stand in Britain and has two terraces with end glazing facing two different pitches – football one side and rugby the other. T-shaped concrete ribs support the roofs of both

stands and allow unimpeded views for spectators. The stand was built as part of a bigger project for Finchley Borough, which also included a lido and other facilities, now sadly demolished.

OLD RECTORY GARDENS, EDGWARE

1932

Welch, Cachemaille-Day and Lander

 Edgware HA8 7LF

This small speculative estate was built opposite the recently opened Edgware tube station and was one of the first set of houses in Metro-Land, and indeed Britain, to use elements of the art deco style in housing. This synthesis between traditional house forms and deco stylings produced the 'Sun Trap' style that quickly spread throughout suburbia. The new elements – white walls, decorative ironwork, curved windows (the sun trap) – lent these new houses a slightly Continental glamour while still embodying the stout principles of British houses: 'no flat roofs here, please'.

ASHLEY LANE

1933

Welch, Cachemaille-Day and Lander

NW4 1HH

WHITE HOUSE, DOWNAGE

1935   Grade II

Evelyn Simmons

NW4 1HP

⊖ both Hendon

A group of flat-roofed houses in Ashley Road and Sherwood Road

in Hendon by Welch, Cachemaille-Day and Lander, now sadly much changed. The houses were similar to some of those by the firm on the Hanger Hill estate (*see Ealing p. 42*), boxy homes in brick with sunroofs and balconies. The most spectacular of the group, No. 54, known as 'Everest', had a curved staircase tower, nautical-style balconies with railings and a sweeping driveway, now unfortunately demolished. One street over is the White House, a striking, Grade II-listed design in white render, with the same components of staircase tower, Crittall windows and sunroof.

BARNET ODEON

1935   Grade II

Edgar Simmons

⊖ High Barnet EN5 1AB

Art deco cinema on the Great North Road in Barnet, which opened in May 1935 and remarkably still operates as a cinema (now for the Everyman chain). Designed in the Moorish style by Edgar Simmons, the interior features green marble columns, a balconied auditorium and Cubist-influenced light fittings. In the street behind, Rayden Road, are a number of speculative semi-detached flat-roofed houses dating from the same time as the cinema.

15

28 SPENCER DRIVE

1934

Welch, Cachemaille-Day and Lander

N2 0QX

LYTTON CLOSE

1935   Grade II

G. G. Winbourne

N2 0RH

 both East Finchley

Hampstead Garden Suburb was founded in 1906 by Henrietta Barnett as one of many planned communities that sprang up in the first part of the twentieth century, and its architecture is heavily influenced by the arts and crafts designs of its planners Barry Parker and Raymond Unwin. There are, however, a number of modernist-influenced houses within its borders. 28 Spencer Drive is a white-rendered, flat-roofed house by Welch, Cachemaille-Day and Lander, with a pantile-edged parapet. The houses in Lytton Close were designed by G. G. Winbourne in a restrained art deco style with curved suntrap windows, glazed staircase towers and sunroofs. There are a number of other modernist houses in the suburb by the likes of Ernst Freud (Neville Road) and Michael Manser (Byron Drive), but many are well hidden by hedges and fences.

HIGHFIELD COURT

1935

A. V. Pilichowski

Brent Cross NW11 9LT

International Style modernist apartment block in Golders Green, which due to its white starkness stands out from the more timid deco-influenced blocks in the neighbourhood. The building, designed by A. V. Pilichowski, is an L-shaped three-storey block with fourteen flats, featuring a sunken garden on one side. Pilichowski was a Polish–Jewish émigré architect who

also collaborated with Berthold Lubetkin on a row of houses in Plumstead. Like many refugees from Europe he anglicised his name, becoming Vivien Pilley during World War II.

2 GOLDERS GREEN ROAD

1936

Ernő Goldfinger

⊖ Golders Green NW11 8LH

One of Ernő Goldfinger's obscurer buildings, 2 Golders Green Road was originally designed in 1935 as a hairdressing salon, but was converted into a shop for S. Weiss ladies' clothing. Situated on a corner of the high street, Goldfinger planned the redesign and rebuild of this site to include a curved glass second floor. Goldfinger also redesigned the interior of the shop and its fittings. Despite now being widely known for his brutalist tower blocks, Goldfinger designed a number of shop interiors during the 1930s.

JOHN KEBLE CHURCH

1936   Grade II

D. F. Martin-Smith

⊖ Edgware HA8 9NT

HENDON METHODIST CHURCH

1937

Welch and Lander

⊖ Hendon NW4 4EH

Two modernist-influenced churches built in the interwar period. John Keble Memorial is just off the M1 motorway in Edgware, and was designed by D. F. Martin-Smith, who won the Edward Maufe-judged competition to build it. The building has a square church tower and is constructed of yellow London stock brick around a reinforced concrete frame, and a ceiling formed using the diagrid method. Hendon Methodist is an expressionist-influenced church in dark brick, designed by Herbert

17

Welch and Felix Lander. The interior features a stained glass window depicting the work of women in the church by Christopher Webb.

BELVEDERE COURT

1938   Grade II

Ernst Freud

⊖ East Finchley N2 0AH

Moderne-style apartment block formed of three long ranges with circular staircase towers, designed by Ernst Freud, son of Sigmund. Intended as rental apartments for Jewish families from Europe, internally the flats were ultra modern, with central heating, fitted kitchens and waste disposal chutes. Ernst had practised architecture in Vienna, and when his family settled in Britain he continued as an architect, designing houses and apartments throughout North London.

EAST FINCHLEY STATION

1939–42   Grade II

Charles Holden and Bucknell and Ellis

N2 0NW

Northern Line station situated awkwardly on a viaduct next to the Great North Road. Originally designed by Leonard Bucknell and Ruth Ellis, the scheme was revised by Charles Holden with construction beginning in 1939 and finally completed in 1942. From street level the exterior doesn't have the visual clarity of earlier 1930s stations, with too many ideas not cohering. However from platform level the station is more interesting, featuring glass staircase towers, a set of offices bridging the tracks and a metal statue of an archer by Eric Aumonier.

BROOKSIDE PRIMARY

1950

Hertfordshire County Council Architects

N14 5NG

OAKLANDS INFANTS

1950   Grade II

Architects Co-Partnership

EN4 8TN

⊖ both Southgate

Two good examples of Hertfordshire County Council's influential post-war school-building programme under C. H. Aslin and Stirrat Johnson-Marshall. An influx of school-age children and lack of facilities from 1945 meant Herts CC had to be creative with its school designs. They employed the

Hills 8' 3" prefab system, allowing schools to be quickly built and flexibly planned, as well as being set on generous plots of land. They employed young, energetic architects like Oliver Cox and David and Mary Medd who designed Brookside Primary (now Monkfrith), as well as firms such as the Architects Co-Partnership who designed Oaklands (now Danegrove).

HOUSES, SPANIARDS END

1959–63   Grade II

Patrick Gwynne

NW3 7JG

HOUSES, BEECHWORTH CLOSE

1961–3

Patrick Gwynne

NW3 7UT

⊖ both Golders Green

Two cul-de-sacs on the edge of Hampstead Garden Suburb featuring houses by Patrick Gwynne. Most well known for his own house, The Homewood in Esher, Gwynne designed a number of private houses in the suburbs around London and the Home Counties in the post-war years. These houses in Barnet show typical Gwynne characteristics: plans that take full advantage of their sites, well-sculpted landscapes and interiors featuring ingenious furniture and fittings. Spaniard's End also features Heathbrow, by H. C. Higgins, with its blank brick facade, praised by Ian Nairn in 1964 as 'one of the most powerful new buildings in London'.

LIBRARY, HALE LANE

1961

B. Bancroft

⊖ Edgware HA8 8NN

Branch library designed in an L shape, featuring a glazed gable end and a copper roof. The building has already been extended once with more refurbishment planned. Bancroft also designed Burnt Oak Library for the borough, a square, concrete, framed building with a glass pyramid roof light and interesting vertical windows, refurbished with a colourful curved entrance way by Knott Architects in 2011. Barnet's libraries, once the pride of the borough, have gradually had their services cut back and face a bleak future, as do many library services throughout London.

ANGEL COTTAGES

1966

R. Seifert and Partners

NW7 1RD

were designed by the firm of Richard Seifert, famous for office buildings like Centrepoint and nearby Ever Ready House, who also lived in the village. Just around the corner is Kingshead, a brick house with multiple sloping roofs by Gerd Kaufmann, reminiscent of his house in Kerry Avenue, Stanmore [see Harrow p. 81].

KINGSHEAD HOUSE

1982

Gerd Kaufmann

NW7 1QX

 both Mill Hill

Mill Hill remains one of the most rural parts of the borough, and the village contains a number of interesting post-war houses. Angel Cottages is a group of four houses overlooking a pond, built in red brick with timber boarding and tiled roofs. They

HENDON HALL COURT

1966

Owen Luder

 Hendon NW4 1QY

Brutalist-style luxury flats designed by the Owen Luder Partnership for developer E. Alec Colman Investments, for whom the firm designed the Tricorn Centre in Portsmouth and Trinity Square car park in Gateshead. The site contains fifty-four flats, in a mixture of two and three bedrooms and maisonettes. The flats, set in the grounds of the Hendon Hall Hotel,

are constructed of reinforced concrete designed to contrast with and become part of the landscaped gardens, bringing a slice of *béton brut* to this corner of Barnet.

ST JOHN'S UNITED REFORMED CHURCH

1967

Jon Finlayson and Iain Langlands

 High Barnet EN5 1RH

Hidden but striking post-war church on a side street in New Barnet. It has a steep slate-lined roof, whose eaves come down to ground level, and long thin windows to draw light in from its awkward position. The building was built to replace the previous church, and one of its architects, Jon Finlayson, was a member of the congregation.

FINCHLEY UNITED SYNAGOGUE

1967

Dowton and Hurst

 Finchley Central N3 3DU

Barnet is home to a number of synagogues, some more modernist than others. Finchley United is a large synagogue overlooking a green next to the North Circular. It was designed by Dowton and Hurst with a front elevation of angled Portland stone and has stained glass work by R. L. Rothschild. Other modernist synagogues in Barnet include the deco Hendon United (1935) by Cecil J. Eprile and the North Western Reform in Golders Green (1936) by Fritz Landauer.

83 WEST HEATH ROAD

1971

Peter Turnbull of Michael Manser Associates

 Golders Green NW3 7TN

One of many post-war modernist houses in this area of Barnet, which takes in Golders Green and Hampstead. Designed by Peter Turnbull of Michael Manser Associates, this house is a one-storey brick building with a prominent steel frame, featuring a glazed central courtyard. Another post-war house with prominent steel construction is 21 West Heath Close (1961) by Anthony Levy, built overlooking Golders Green Park. It has a pleasingly simple design, consisting of a one-storey rectangular box, supported at one end by thin steel columns. Unfortunately, at time of writing, it is looking very dilapidated.

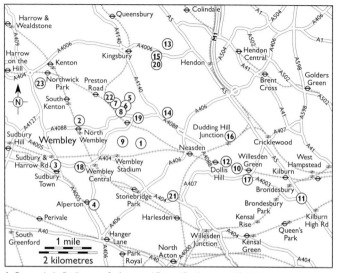

1. Former India Pavilion
2. Wrigley's Factory
3. Sudbury Town Station
4. Alperton Station
5. Barn Rise
6. Mayfields
7. The Avenue
8. Lawns Court
9. Arena and Empire Pool
10. Kingsley Court
11. Gaumont State Cinema
12. Sherrick Green Road School
13. Highfort Court
14. Old St Andrews Mansions
15. Slough Lane
16. Dollis Hill Synagogue
17. Willesden Green
    Federated Synagogue
18. Wembley Fire Station
19. Wembley Town Hall
20. Ferndene Apartments
21. Five Precious Wounds
22. Church of the Ascension
23. Northwick Park Hospital

BRENT

Brent has an interesting architectural history, split between the urban southern part featuring Willesden and Kilburn, which developed first, and the more rural northern areas at Wembley and Kingsbury. Wembley is the most significant area in terms of modernist design, being the place used for attracting people out to the suburbs, first through the failed Watkin's Tower and then the more successful British Empire Exhibition of 1924–5. The exhibition was modern in construction rather than design, with the Owen Williams-planned reinforced concrete structures such as the Palace of Engineering paving the way for his more radical Empire Pool on the same site a decade later. The influx of visitors to the exhibition, 25 million by the time it closed, also provided a population boom resulting in modernist-style homes, designed by Welch, Cachemaille-Day and Lander for the Haymills Ltd, being built on the slopes of Wembley.

At the same time as those flat-roofed houses were appearing, Ernest Trobridge was producing more historically inspired designs in Kingsbury. Like the exhibition buildings, designs like Trobridge's flats on Highfield Avenue hid contemporary reinforced-concrete construction. Like most of the boroughs featured in this book, Brent has a few underground stations by Charles Holden. At Sudbury Town, Holden produced his breakthrough box design that he spent the next decade refining. Post war, the progressive interwar legacy was not taken on, with local authority housing like the Chalkhill Estate, Wembley being quickly built and equally quickly torn down. Also demolished were the buildings of the Empire Exhibition, now only remembered by the India Pavilion, turned into a warehouse.

FORMER INDIA PAVILION

1924

Charles Allom and Sons

⊖ Wembley Park HA9 0JD

One of the last surviving fragments of the British Empire Exhibition of 1924–5. Originally the building imitated Indian designs such as the Taj Mahal and acted as the Indian Pavilion

at the exhibition, giving visitors a flavour of the subcontinent. Now minus its dome and towers, it has been converted into a warehouse, a fate which befell most of the exhibition buildings before their eventual demolition. Until 2013, the Palace of Industry also survived. Designed by Owen Williams and Maxwell Ayrton, this exhibition hall covered ten acres, with imposing classical entrances and large glazed roofs supported by concrete walls. A decorative lion's head from the Palace of Industry has been saved and relocated to Wembley Hill Road.

WRIGLEY'S FACTORY

1928

Wallis, Gilbert and Partners

⊖ North Wembley HA9 7UR

Many of the earliest modernist buildings in Metro-Land, and indeed Britain, were functional buildings such as factories and stadiums. This factory building is a good example. More subdued than the firm's designs on the Great West Road [*see Hounslow p. 96*], the firm of Wallis, Gilbert and Partners built a four-storey factory for the American Wrigley's chewing gum company in 1928. The interior was designed to be rearranged to allow for changes in production, with the ceilings supported by circular mushroom pillars. The building has now been converted into a commercial centre.

SUDBURY TOWN STATION

1931   Grade II*

Charles Holden

HA0 2LA

ALPERTON STATION

1933

Charles Holden and Stanley Heaps

HA0 4LU

Sudbury Town is the original 'Sudbury Box' design by Holden, described in his own words as 'a brick box with a concrete lid'. Indeed the building is constructed from multi-coloured handmade Buckinghamshire brick, with a poured concrete roof. The outside originally featured a neon name sign, the only tube station to have one, removed in 1958. Compared to later box-style buildings like Oakwood or Acton Town, Sudbury

Town has limited window space, with four long Crittall windows allowing light into the ticket hall. Inside the ticket hall the original clock and barometer survive, as well as a newspaper kiosk. The platform area features two curved waiting areas, designed to allow passengers to see incoming trains, and a concrete footbridge. Sudbury Town is in a lot of ways Holden's ideal design. He spent the next decade refining it, in built and unbuilt stations.

Brent is also home to Alperton station, again by Holden, who used the box design at right angles to a viaduct, with a steep passenger staircase. The station had an escalator used in the Dome of Discovery at the Festival of Britain installed in 1955, which is still in place but bricked in by a wall. Stanley Heaps designed the adjacent bus depot, which was completed in 1938.

BARN RISE

1932

HA9 9NN

MAYFIELDS

1934

HA9 9PD

THE AVENUE

1934

HA9 9PQ

LAWNS COURT

1933

HA9 9PD

all Welch, Cachemaille-Day and Lander

 all Wembley Park

Among more traditional designs, an interesting selection of modernist-influenced speculative housing dots the slopes of Wembley, all designed by the firm of Welch, Cachemaille-Day and Lander for the Haymills development company. In Barn Rise are four detached houses in brick with pantiled roof parapets. Further down the hill is Lawns Court, six three-storey blocks of flats in white render with curving exterior staircases. In the adjacent road, Mayfields, and along The Avenue are three-storey houses with sunroofs, perfect examples of the International Style brought to the English suburbs.

ARENA AND EMPIRE POOL

1934   Grade II

Owen Williams

 Wembley Park HA9 0AA

Built ten years after his work on the Empire Exhibition buildings and the Empire Stadium [the original Wembley Stadium], Williams' design for the

1934 Empire Games shows a leap forward in design. This structure, featuring three concrete span arches measuring seventy-two metres with exterior supporting fins, and boxy

water towers, has a fortress-like air. Despite this it has come to be somewhat of a national treasure after its conversion to a popular concert venue, and marks the high point of Williams' journey from engineer to architect.

KINGSLEY COURT

1934   Grade II

Peter Caspari

⊖ Willesden Green NW2 5TJ

An expressionist apartment block alongside the Metropolitan Line designed by Peter Caspari. The building is six storeys high and built in banded brick that curves with an assurance not seen in other buildings of its period. Caspari was one of many émigré architects to flee to Britain from Europe in the 1920s and 1930s. As with many of those who came here, like Erich Mendelsohn, whom

he had assisted, Caspri only stayed for a few years before moving over the other side of the Atlantic. Kingsley Court represents the best of Caspari's brief stay.

GAUMONT STATE CINEMA

1937   Grade II*

George Coles

 Kilburn NW6 7HY

Towering former cinema designed by the prolific George Coles. Coles produced nearly ninety cinemas in the interwar period, with designs all over Metro-Land. This cinema is a good example of the 'more is more' style of cinema design, in which the building acts as an advert for itself, an idea not so different from Charles Holden's underground stations. The Gaumont State Kilburn has central tower finished in cream-coloured faience and a lobby that is panelled with green vitrolite. Like many surviving cinema buildings in London, it became a bingo hall before converting to a church.

SHERRICK GREEN ROAD SCHOOL

1937

Wilkinson, Rowe and Johnson-Marshall

Dollis Hill NW10 1LB

Now known as Gladstone Park, this school was built to designs by Wilkinson, Rowe and Johnson-Marshall for the Borough of Willesden architects department. The school has an unusual shape, being long and thin, with prominent staircase towers at each end of the building. The trio of architects also designed the now demolished, moderne Electricity Showrooms in Willesden. Stirrat Johnson-Marshall would go on to form RMJM, now one of the world's largest architectural firms.

HIGHFORT COURT

1937

Kingsbury NW9 0QG

OLD ST ANDREWS MANSIONS

1936   Grade II

 Wembley Park NW9 8TD

SLOUGH LANE

1922   Grade II

 Kingsbury NW9 8XL

all Ernest Trobridge

Certainly not modernist, but the epitome of the spirit of Metro-Land and the idea that 'an Englishman's home is his castle'. Trobridge's Swedenborgian religion informed his belief in the healing properties of design, especially for those returning from World War I. His most famous building is Highfort Court, with its fantastical turreted entrance, as perched upon by John Betjeman in his *Metro-Land* documentary. Trobridge used a variety of materials including elm, thatch, tiles and even concrete. His designs can be found all over the slopes of Kingsbury, bringing a taste of the middle ages to Metro-Land.

DOLLIS HILL SYNAGOGUE

1933–8   Grade II

Owen Williams

 Dollis Hill NW2 6RJ

Stark, concrete synagogue and hall on the edge of Gladstone Park, designed for the United Synagogue. The buildings are constructed of prestressed concrete folded slabs and have hexagonal and shield-shaped windows, creating another fortress-like structure as at the Empire Pool. Unlike that building, Williams' design here was not judged a success, with the architect forced to pay back some of the fee to his clients. Nevertheless it is now Grade II and still in use, now as a Jewish primary school.

WILLESDEN GREEN FEDERATED SYNAGOGUE

1938

Fritz Landauer

 Willesden Green NW2 5JE

A slightly more approachable synagogue design by Fritz Landauer, just off Willesden Lane. The building is constructed of brick and originally had decorative ironwork grills above the entrance. Now in use as an advice centre, the brick has been rendered and the ironwork removed. Landauer was another European émigré, fleeing Germany in 1933. He designed another synagogue in Golders Green and a number of commercial properties, and stayed in Britain for the rest of his life.

WEMBLEY FIRE STATION

1939   Grade II

Cecil S. Trapp and Middlesex County Council

 Wembley Central HA0 2EG

Fire station built just before World War II in Buckinghamshire brick with a reinforced concrete frame. This interwar station was designed by the Borough of Wembley surveyor Cecil S. Trapp, with Middlesex County Council under C. G. Stillman making extensions and alterations in 1954, adding a third floor to the station building and a dormitory block at the rear. The building still features the original stained timber doors in the fire station bays.

WEMBLEY TOWN HALL

1940   Grade II

Clifford Strange

Wembley Park HA9 9LY

One of a number of town halls built in suburban borough centres in the interwar years. This slightly austere brick building sits on a sloping site on Forty Lane overlooking the former Empire Exhibition site. Clifford Strange won the competition to design an administrative building for Wembley Urban District Council with a Scandinavian-influenced building that includes offices, a library and an assembly chamber. Despite the sober exterior, the interior features Botticino marble flooring and staircase railings of silver bronze. In 2013 Brent Council sold the building to an international school and moved their offices to a new building on the former exhibition site.

FERNDENE APARTMENTS

1965

Clifford Wearden and Partners

⊖ Kingsbury NW9 8XL

Sitting opposite Ernest Trobridge's rustic Slough Lane cottages, this retirement complex is separated chronologically from them by forty years, and in spirit by a couple of centuries. Planned around mature trees, this scheme has a mixture of housing sizes, all featuring an underground garage to separate traffic from pedestrians. The entrance features a long sloping shuttered concrete access ramp.

Five Precious Wounds is a brutalist-style church in red brick designed by John Newton of Burles, Newton and Partners. The church building features long windows strips with stained glass, with a presbytery and church hall included as part of the complex. A more traditional style church can be found at the Church of the Ascension, Wembley. It was the last church designed by Harold Gibbons

FIVE PRECIOUS WOUNDS

1967

Burles, Newton and Partners

 Harlesden NW10 8ER

CHURCH OF THE ASCENSION

1957   Grade II

J. Harold Gibbons

Wembley Park HA9 9QL

and the outside is in Gibbons' favoured Gothic Revival in stock brick. Inside, the whitewashed walls allow the altar mural by Hans Feibusch and stained glass work by W. T. Carter Shapland, among others, to shine.

NORTHWICK PARK HOSPITAL

1969–75

Llewelyn-Davies, Weeks, Forestier-Walker and Bor

Northwick Park HA1 3UJ

Large brutalist hospital on the northern edge of Brent. It was built between 1969 and 1975, and designed by John Weeks, with engineering by Ove Arup and Partners. The idea behind the design was to allow flexibility for expansion of medical services over time as technology changes. To achieve this the scheme is arranged in a street system with buildings able to change purpose and be extended as needed. The style of the buildings is very much of its time, with heavy use of both prefab and in situ concrete elements, and an irregular arrangement of windows throughout.

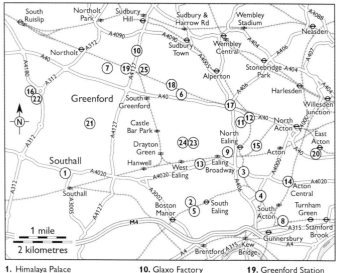

1. Himalaya Palace
2. Ealing Odeon
3. Ealing Common Station
4. Acton Town Station
5. Northfields Station
6. Hoover Factory and Canteen
7. Aladdin Factory
8. Chiswick Park Station
9. Ealing Village
10. Glaxo Factory
11. Hanger Hill Estate
12. Park Royal Station
13. Longfield House
14. Acton Granada
15. West Acton Station
16. Prefabs, Edward Road
17. Hanger Lane Station
18. Perivale Station
19. Greenford Station
20. St Aidan
21. Christ the Redeemer
22. St Joseph the Worker
23. The Grange and
    White Ledges
24. Children's Home
25. IBM Greenford

EALING

The Borough of Ealing, much like Brent and Barnet, was until the first half of the twentieth century split between a more urban southern half, and a rural northern half. Towns like Acton and Ealing rose to prominence in the Victorian era, with Ealing earning the sobriquet 'Queen of the Suburbs'. Consequently much of the architecture in these areas is made up of Victorian and Edwardian-era buildings, with rows of terraces making up much of the housing stock. When modernist design did emerge it tended to be used for buildings such as cinemas or factories in the more industrial areas like Acton. Conversely the more rural areas such as Perivale, Greenford and Northolt were ripe for more expansive building. The Hanger Hill estate provided a fairly blank canvas for Welch, Cachemaille-Day and Lander to design houses, a hotel and a tube station.

The underground was not the only mode of transport that brought modernism to the suburbs. The building of new arterial roads such as Western Avenue provided room for art deco factories by Wallis, Gilbert and Partners, whose Hoover Building has become such a fixture of the London end of the A40. Ealing has its fair share of Charles Holden stations, but perhaps more interesting are the Central Line stations, designed before World War II and built afterwards. Ealing Council didn't produce much in the way of high quality designs after becoming a borough in 1965, but there are a number of impressive post-war buildings in the area. West London has many post-war churches, with a few examples in Ealing by Maguire and Murray and Michael Farey, and Greenford has a high-tech office and warehouse building by Norman Foster for IBM.

HIMALAYA PALACE

1928   Grade II*

George Coles

⊖ Southall UB1 1RT

EALING ODEON

1932   Grade II*

Cecil Masey

⊖ Northfields W5 4UB

Two great examples of the use of exotic detailing in interwar cinema design. Howard Carter's discovery of Tutankhamun's tomb in 1922 led to a wave in Egyptian-themed design, as seen in cinemas and factories of the period. Other cultures were in turn plundered for their details. The Himalaya Palace in Southall was originally designed by George Coles for the United Picture Theatres' chain and made to look like a Chinese pagoda, complete with red tiled roof and dragon gargoyles. By contrast the Ealing Odeon by Cecil Masey uses a Moorish theme, with white rendered walls and ornate tilework on the exterior, and a tented ceiling and hanging lamps inside. As with most cinemas these buildings now serve other functions; the Himalaya Palace

is an indoor market and the Ealing Odeon a church.

EALING COMMON STATION

1931   Grade II

Charles Holden and Stanley Heaps

W5 3NU

ACTON TOWN STATION

1932   Grade II

Charles Holden

W3 8HN

NORTHFIELDS STATION

1932   Grade II

Charles Holden and Stanley Heaps

W5 4UB

A trio of underground stations that show the leap in design Charles Holden made at the start of the 1930s. Ealing Common has a heptagonal ticket hall clad in Portland stone, reminiscent of his Northern Line stations of the mid-1920s, part way

between Victorian grandiosity and the coming modernity. Acton Town employs the 'Sudbury Box' model; a rectangular ticket hall in Buckinghamshire brick with double-height windows. Northfields repeats the trick, albeit slightly less successfully, with a rotated ticket hall. Holden wouldn't make such a giant leap in design again; however, he would introduce the circle alongside the square to great effect.

HOOVER FACTORY

1932–5   Grade II*

CANTEEN BLOCK

1938   Grade II*

both Wallis, Gilbert and Partners

⊖ both Perivale UB6 8DW

One of the most distinctive buildings along Western Avenue, this factory for Hoover is an Egyptian-inspired art deco monument that has divided critics throughout the years. Wallis, Gilbert and Partners designed ten separate buildings for this project, with the most interesting and eye-catching being the main front block and the canteen block. The main block is 220 feet long with generous glazing and decoration in coloured tiles. At either end are two staircase towers with quarter-moon windows inspired by the work of Erich Mendelsohn.

The three-storey canteen and garage block was designed and built later than the main block, in 1938. It is constructed of reinforced concrete, and features a long, vertical, V-shaped window at the front. After Hoover left in the 1980s, Tesco took over the buildings, converting the rear into a supermarket and letting out offices in the front. The main block has now been converted into apartments.

ALADDIN FACTORY

1931–2

C. Nicholas and J. E. Dixon-Spain

🚇 Greenford UB6 8LZ

Former factory built for Aladdin Industries on Western Avenue, with a campanile-style bell tower. The factory was designed by the partnership of Charles Nicholas and John Edward Dixon-Spain, who designed a variety of buildings in the interwar period. Perhaps more interesting than his design career are Dixon-Spain's adventures in World War II. He was one of the original 'Monuments Men', charged with saving precious works of art in the hands of the Nazis from being destroyed, later immortalised in a film featuring George Clooney. The building has been given over to retail in recent years.

CHISWICK PARK STATION

1933   Grade II

Charles Holden with Stanley Heaps

W4 5NE

As mentioned previously, here Holden introduces the curve to go with the right angle. As at Arnos Grove [*see Enfield pp. 50–51*] a semicircular ticket hall sits on a square base with a structure of multi-coloured brick and areas of exposed concrete inside, with the addition of a squat brick tower. The station was designed by Charles Holden, but as with many stations of the era, Stanley Heaps was responsible for overseeing the construction

and alterations as needed. Heaps was responsible for the cantilevered concrete canopies on the platform, also seen at many other stations on the Piccadilly Line.

EALING VILLAGE

1934   Grade II

R. Toms and Partners

 North Ealing W5 2LZ

Dutch colonial-inspired, private estate, built to attract film stars from the nearby Ealing Studios. Designed by the firm R. Toms and Partners, this village is similar to Elm Park Court and Pinner Court [*see Harrow p. 74*] in trying to bring some Sunset Boulevard glamour to the suburbs with its whitewashed walls, green pantiles and mansard roofs. The estate also features a swimming pool, tennis court, clubhouse, bowling green and a croquet lawn. The Ealing Hollywood did not really come to fruition, with

most of the apartments bought by film crew rather than screen stars. It still remains as a reminder of the brief glory days of the British film industry.

GLAXO FACTORY

1935   Grade II

Wallis, Gilbert and Partners

 Greenford UB6 0HQ

After the fireworks of the Hoover factory, something slightly more down to earth from Wallis, Gilbert and Partners.

The Glaxo complex featured offices, labs and factory buildings, with the main administrative and research blocks built of brown brick around a steel frame. It was built on a site next to the Grand Union Canal to allow materials to be bought by boat. The main block has a strong horizontal emphasis, accentuated by brick bands and continuous concrete lintel that stretch around the front of the building. Like the Hoover factory, this site is being converted into housing and shops.

HANGER HILL ESTATE

1934–36

Welch, Cachemaille-Day and Lander

⊖ Park Royal W5 3ER

Estate just off Western Avenue, designed by Welch, Cachemaille-Day and Lander for the Haymills construction company. The estate is formed

of concentric half-crescent streets starting with Hanger Court, a curved block of flats. The houses are a mixture of styles, with more traditional designs alongside modernist houses

with sunroofs. The best selection of modernist houses are along The Ridings. Also as part of the estate the firm designed the Park Royal Hotel, featuring a bar/hotel, garage and shops built in yellow and red brick, with distinctive twisted brick columns. The building has been through several changes of owners and functions, and is undergoing redevelopment.

PARK ROYAL STATION

1936   Grade II

Welch and Lander

W5 3EL

Station built to serve the new Hanger Hill estate and the factories of Park Royal. Designed by Herbert Welch and Felix Lander rather than Charles Holden, this station keeps to the high London Underground standard of the 1930s. It is built in brick with a double-height circular booking hall, square tower and an adjoining three-storey building containing shops and flats. Viewed from platform level, the building steps up to street level in a series of shapes, giving the station a Cubist air.

LONGFIELD HOUSE

1936

Ernest Schaufelberg

Ealing Broadway W5 2SR

A modernist block of flats designed by Ernest Schaufelberg on the Uxbridge Road in Ealing. Schaufelberg is best known for designing West End theatres such as the Adelphi and the Fortune. Art deco apartment blocks of the interwar years are often compared to ocean liners. This one is more like a destroyer, with its various staircases, balconies, railings and terraces, all in steel and stark white reinforced concrete.

ACTON GRANADA

1937   Grade II

F. E. Bromige

Acton Central W3 6LJ

Cinema building that opened as the Dominion Cinema in 1937. Designed by F. E. Bromige, the building is dominated by a curved glass frontage, with wrought iron balconies and thin concrete support fins. It was taken over by the Granada circuit in 1946 and continued as a cinema until 1972, when it became a bingo club. Since then it has been a church and an indoor activity centre.

43

WEST ACTON STATION

1940   Grade II

Brian Lewis

W3 0DS

The first Central Line station designed by Australian architect Brian Lewis and the only one completed to his designs. Lewis was the chief architect for Great Western Railways, who built and ran the western extension Central Line stations for London Underground. This station has a glass-brick frontage sandwiched between two brick end walls, and is an interesting variation on the Holden box formula. The platforms feature lovely original shelters with wooden benches.

PREFABS, EDWARD ROAD, NORTHOLT

1945

Frederick Gibberd

 Northolt UB5 6QW

After World War II, Britain faced a chronic lack of housing, as well as depleted manpower and materials. To overcome this, the wartime government began researching prefabricated housing. Many different models were produced and built, including the British Iron and Steel Federation (BISF) House, designed by Frederick Gibberd, constructed of a steel frame with brick-and-timber infill. Despite its prefabricated nature it was

designed to be a permanent house, and many can still be found across the London suburbs, particularly next to the North Circular Road.

HANGER LANE STATION

1947

W5 1DL

PERIVALE STATION

1947

UB6 8AE

GREENFORD STATION

1947

UB6 8PX

all Brian Lewis and F. F. C. Curtis

Three more stations designed by Brian Lewis for the Central Line. They were all planned before World War II, but not built until afterwards. In the meantime, due to material and labour shortages, the designs were reworked by Lewis' successor Frederick Curtis. These reworkings usually meant removing a tower or reducing the height of the ticket hall. Of the three, the most interesting is Hanger Lane with its circular form, echoing Arnos Grove station. Unfortunately the Hanger Lane gyratory has ended up obscuring the building from all but the most ardent searcher. Perivale and Greenford are similar designs with their curving brick frontages at right angles to the railway line.

ST AIDAN

1961

Burles, Newton and Partners

⊖ East Acton W3 7DD

CHRIST THE REDEEMER

1964

Michael A. Farey

 Southall UB1 2HE

ST JOSEPH THE WORKER

1969

Maguire and Murray

 Northolt UB5 6JS

Ealing, like most of the western suburbs, is home to a variety of post-war church designs. St Aidan in East Acton has a plain exterior but a wealth of artworks inside; a crucifixion by Graham Sutherland, a baptistery by Adam Kossowski and *dalle de verre* glass by Pierre Fourmaintraux. Elsewhere there is Christ the Redeemer, Southall, with a large curved window and open bell cage and the brutalist St Joseph the Worker in Northolt by Maguire and Murray.

THE GRANGE

1965

Kenneth Bland for Wates Ltd

WHITE LEDGES

1968

Derek Lovejoy and Partners

 both Ealing Broadway W13 8JB

Two phases of an estate in Ealing built on the sites of former country houses, influenced by Eric Lyons' work for Span Developments [*see Richmond*]. The Grange estate was built by the construction and development company Wates Ltd and designed by their in-house architect Kenneth Bland. It is arranged around a lake, with two ten-storey point blocks, a two-storey apartment block and seventy-eight houses. Most of the houses have typical mid-century tile hanging, as well as integral garages. The second phase, White Ledges, was designed by Derek Lovejoy and Partners, known for their well-landscaped designs, and features terraced townhouses with roof gardens.

CHILDREN'S HOME

1970

Yorke, Rosenberg and Mardall

 Ealing Broadway W13 8HH

Residential home for children designed for Westminster City Council by Yorke, Rosenberg and Mardall. The building had a mixture of facilities including bedrooms, kitchens, play areas and utility rooms. The building has a brick ground floor supporting a cantilevered concrete first floor, which acts as a part shelter for the playground. After a period of dereliction it has been redeveloped as a sixth-form centre for a nearby school.

IBM GREENFORD

1980   Grade II

Norman Foster and Partners

 Greenford UB6 0AD

High-tech warehouse complex originally designed by Norman Foster and Partners for IBM, now part occupied by the Royal Mail. Formed of two main buildings, a distribution centre and a display hall, the complex is a perfect example of the 1970s high-tech style, with aluminium cladding, glass walls and brightly coloured detailing. Like the interwar factories of Owen Williams and Wallis, Gilbert and Partners, the interiors are designed to be flexibly planned, allowing for changes in workflow or technology.

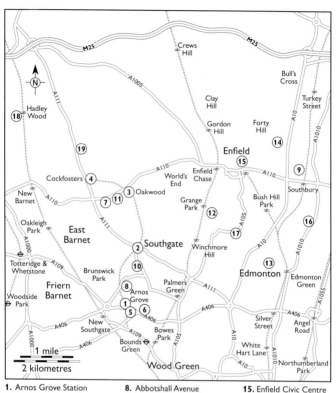

1. Arnos Grove Station
2. Southgate Station
3. Oakwood Station
4. Cockfosters Station
5. Bowes Road Clinic
6. Caretaker's House
7. De Bohun School, Library and Clinic
8. Abbotshall Avenue
9. Ripaults Factory
10. Ellington Court
11. Christ the King
12. Grange Park Methodist Church
13. Edmonton Fire Station
14. Queen Elizabeth II Stadium
15. Enfield Civic Centre
16. St Alphege Church and Vicarage
17. Ridge Avenue Library
18. Bartrams Lane
19. Water Tower

ENFIELD

Like many of the other boroughs in this book, Enfield has an industrial half and a more suburban half. The industrial area takes in Edmonton and parts of Enfield, with the more suburban area between Southgate and Grange Park. Until the start of the twentieth century, Enfield was quite rural. But with the extension of the railways and the building of the Great Northern Road, factories and houses came quickly to the area. Architecturally, Enfield has many interesting modernist buildings, particularly those built for the public good – schools, libraries, health clinics and tube stations. Indeed, in the Piccadilly Line stations of Arnos Grove and Southgate, it has two of the best modernist buildings in the country. Elsewhere are great examples of the work of Curtis and Burchett for Middlesex County Council between the wars, of which Enfield was the eastern boundary until 1965.

Post World War II, Curtis and Burchett's work was continued by C. G. Stillman, who designed a number of schools in the borough. The pre-1965 Edmonton Borough architects' department under T. A. Wilkinson was also quite radical for its time, building new housing in precast concrete panels with a direct labour organisation, something that boroughs like Camden would take on in the 1960s and 1970s. There are also some good examples of the differing scales of post-war modernism: a monolithic concrete water tower in Cockfosters by the firm of Scherrer and Hicks, and nearby, on a smaller scale, some flat-roofed houses in Hadley Wood by Donald and Mary Craig.

ARNOS GROVE STATION

1932   Grade II*

N11 1AN

SOUTHGATE STATION

1933   Grade II*

N14 5BH

both Charles Holden

We start at the top, with two of the best modernist buildings in Britain, let alone Metro-Land. These stations were part of the Piccadilly Line extension to Cockfosters [*see Haringey p. 61*] and perfectly illustrate Charles Holden's balance between modernism and arts and crafts; simple, functional, design with considered use of local materials. Arnos Grove is formed of a circular booking hall on a square base, designed to allow passenger flow and creating an impressive interior space. A single concrete pillar supports the roof, with the original passimeter ticket office still at the base.

One of Holden's most distinctive stations, Southgate is a low circular structure, often compared to a UFO. The roof tapers to a point and is topped with five circular lights that slide open and shut, with a ball on top. Inside, as at Arnos Grove, a single concrete pole supports the roof, with a passimeter at the base. There is an integrated bus station, with a long, curved, shopping parade, allowing buses to circulate into the station from the road. The exterior also features the wonderful masts that were designed to combine lighting, seating and timetables.

OAKWOOD STATION

1933   Grade II*

C. H. James

N14 4UT

COCKFOSTERS STATION

1933   Grade II

Charles Holden

EN4 0DZ

Initially called Enfield West, before being renamed Oakwood in 1946, this station was designed by C. H. James in a simple 'Sudbury Box' design. It is reminiscent of Acton Town, but with a larger canopy at the front. A bus station had been intended as part of the design but was dropped due to low passenger numbers. The platform features cantilevered concrete canopies, designed by Stanley Heaps. C. H. James was an architect better known for his house designs, especially in Welwyn Garden City.

Cockfosters is the end of the Piccadilly line extension, originally

planned as a much grander terminus-style building, with towers either side of the road. It is one of Holden's stations where the beauty is underground, much like Gants Hill. The station features a long low station building, with a subway entrance opposite. The ticket hall and platform areas are often likened to a church, due to the long nave-like shape and clerestory windows. The use of plain, board-marked concrete points the way to post-war architectural styles such as brutalism. The original plan allowed for an extension to incorporate two parades of shops, a staff building, a garage and even potentially a cinema. However the expected passenger traffic did not materialise, and the station remains as opened in 1933.

The Bowes Road complex, which features a swimming pool, library and health centre, was designed and built between 1935 and 1940, designed by Curtis and Burchett for Middlesex County Council. The heavy influence of Dutch architecture, in particular Willem Dudok, can be seen here, especially in the design for the library with its central staircase tower and brown brick construction. The swimming pool is a single-storey building with an oval foyer and a circular concrete skylight. The medical clinic was completed last of the three buildings, and is laid out in an L-shape plan that steps upwards to a tall brick chimney. Just around the corner is the squat brick caretaker's house to Broomfield School, another Curtis and Burchett design.

BOWES ROAD CLINIC

1935–40   Grade II

N11 1BD

CARETAKER'S HOUSE

1938

both Curtis and Burchett

both Arnos Grove N14 7HX

DE BOHUN SCHOOL, LIBRARY AND CLINIC

1936–9   Grade II

Curtis and Burchett

Oakwood N14 4AD

More Middlesex County Council modernism, with a site that combines a school, library and clinic, typical of the interwar idea of combined services. The school was built first, and has a heavily horizontal emphasis with windows and continuous concrete cornices across the first and second floor. This horizontality is punctured by the ubiquitous staircase tower. Next door is the library and health clinic building (now a nursery school), also in red brick, with stepped floors around the central tower, and heavy overhanging eaves.

ABBOTSHALL AVENUE

1936

Frank Woodward

 Arnos Grove N14 7JU

A group of nine art deco-style houses designed by Frank Woodward, who along with his brother Charles also acted as developer for the scheme. As with many modernist speculative houses from the interwar period, they were built in brick and rendered white to give the impression of concrete. This was often done as at the time, many smaller building firms did not have the requisite technical expertise to build in concrete. Nearby in

Whitehouse Way (actually in Barnet) is another group of flat-roofed, streamline houses probably built for the Davis Estates company.

RIPAULTS FACTORY

1936   Grade II

A. H. Durnford

 Southbury EN1 1TH

One of the only remaining modernist examples of Enfield's many factories and industrial buildings from the first half of the twentieth century. This factory, originally built for the Ripaults cable company, has a sleek, streamlined style with a long horizontal building and a short rectangular tower, along with chrome strips and black trim for decoration. The many

factories and industrial sites that lined the Great Cambridge Road and others have gradually been demolished and replaced with retail parks and offices since the 1980s.

ELLINGTON COURT

1936

Frederick Gibberd

 Southgate N14 6LB

An early project by architect Frederick Gibberd, these luxury flats on Southgate High Street are built in brick with prominent curving concrete entrance canopies. When built, the interior featured central heating, marble fireplaces and sliding doors. Unfortunately the building has recently had an extra floor added, which somewhat detracts from the original design.

CHRIST THE KING

1940

Constantine Bosschaerts

⊖ Oakwood N14 4HE

GRANGE PARK METHODIST CHURCH

1938

C. H. Brightliff

⊖ Grange Park N21 2EU

Monastery building that was founded and designed by Dom Constantine Bosschaerts, a Belgian monk, who had practiced as an architect before joining the Benedictine order. The building, which is only a small part of the original overall design, was completed in 1940 and consists of

a reinforced concrete frame filled with white brick, and a tower with an eye-catching recessed red cross. Bosschaerts died in 1950 and subsequent extensions to the complex were made by his successor Dom Placid Meylink. Over in Grange Park is a Methodist church by C. H. Brighliff with a striking art deco tower.

EDMONTON FIRE STATION

1941

Edmonton Architects Department

 Edmonton Green N9 9AA

Fire station building with a long, plain frontage and circular end towers. Designed by Edmonton architects' department in a pared-down deco style, the station also has stone window bands and surrounds. Edmonton Borough were one of the more proactive municipal architect departments. Led by T. A. Wilkinson (who would go

on to become chief architect for Enfield), they designed and built health centres, schools, clinics and housing, often using a direct labour organisation for construction and system-built structures before they were widespread.

QUEEN ELIZABETH II STADIUM

1939–53   Grade II

Frank Lee

 Southbury EN1 3PL

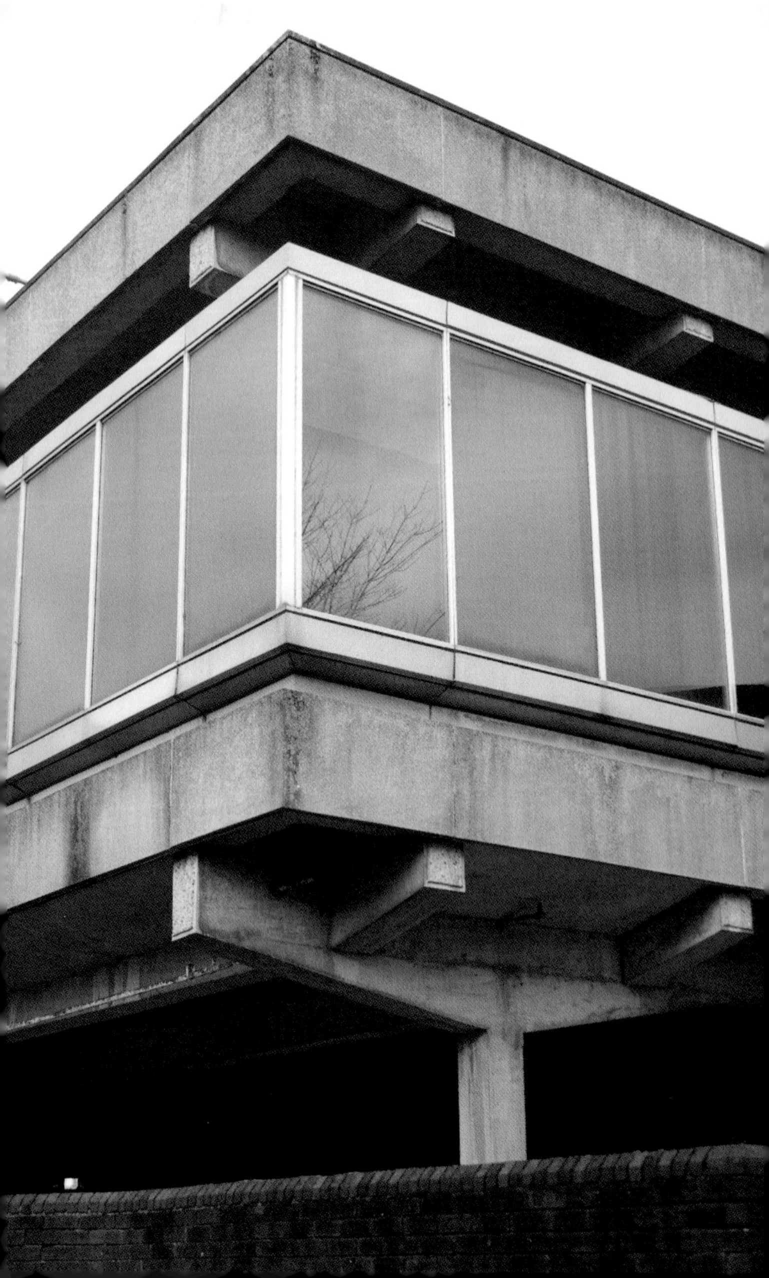

Sports stadium in Enfield, designed in 1939 by Frank Lee, the Edmonton Borough surveyor, but not completed until 1953 due to the outbreak of World War II. The building has a lovely streamline moderne style, as seen in the curved brick drum tower at the east end of the stand, which is supported by a reinforced concrete frame. To complete the 1930s feel, the building features overhanging concrete eaves, Crittall windows and metal railings.

ENFIELD CIVIC CENTRE

1957–75

Eric Broughton and Associates

 Enfield Town EN1 3XA

One of many civic centres built around London in the 1960s and 1970s. It was constructed in two phases, showing the changes in post-war modernist design. The first section

was built 1957–61, and consists of a Scandinavian-influenced administration block in blue and yellow brick overlooking a reflecting pool. The second phase, built between 1972–5, added a brutalist office/car park combination and a striking twelve-storey steel-clad tower. A number of new civic centres were built throughout London's suburbs after the war to accommodate the newly formed boroughs, with many now being redeveloped for housing and their services moved elsewhere.

ST ALPHEGE CHURCH AND VICARAGE, EDMONTON

1958–61   Grade II

Edward Maufe

Ponders End N9 7DH

Church built in pale brick around a portal frame, and designed by Edward Maufe, best known for Guildford Cathedral. The building is influenced by Scandinavian modernism and has a slender bell tower with a statue of St Alphege, a crucifixion relief on the east exterior wall, and a plain interior with a prominent crucifixion painting by C. Pearson. The site also features a vicarage by Maufe and distinctive iron gates.

RIDGE AVENUE LIBRARY

1963

Brian van Breda for Edmonton Architects Department

Bush Hill Park N21 2RH

Branch library designed for Edmonton Borough by in-house architect Brian van Breda. The building features a hyperbolic paraboloid roof, covered in copper on the outside and timber on the inside with floor to ceiling windows, creating a light and open space inside. The scheme also originally featured a health clinic, designed in a similar Scandinavian post-war style. Unfortunately that has now been demolished, and the library also looks in need of some rejuvenation.

and have an interesting arrangement of windows, varying in shape and size around each house. The houses were designed by Donald and Mary Craig, a married couple who worked for Coventry and Stevenage development corporations before setting up in practice for themselves, producing work for local councils like Haringey and Enfield.

BARTRAMS LANE

1964

Donald and Mary Craig

⊖ Hadley Wood EN4 0EH

A small, quiet group of four detached houses tucked away behind Hadley Wood station. The houses are flat roofed, in brick with timber cladding,

WATER TOWER, COCKFOSTERS

1968

Edmund Percey and J. W. Milne

 Cockfosters EN4 0JF

A spectacular concrete water tower, tucked away just off the Cockfosters Road, just a five-minute walk from the station. It is designed with an interlaced hyperbolic lattice to support the water tank and a slender central pipe section. The architects were Edmund Percey and J. W. Milne; Percey worked for the firm of Scherrer and Hicks, noted for their designs of water towers, and Milne was chief engineer of Lee Valley Water.

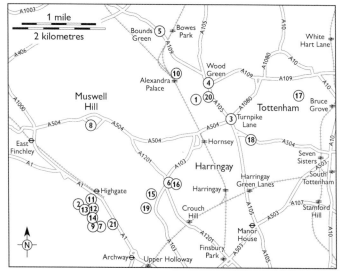

1. Barratt Chocolate Factory
2. Highpoint I and II
3. Turnpike Lane Station
4. Wood Green Station
5. Bounds Green Station
6. Hornsey Town Hall
7. Cholmeley Lodge

8. Muswell Hill Odeon
9. Studio, Duke's Head Yard
10. Haringey Civic Centre
11. Southwood House Estate
12. Southwood Park
13. 99–109 Southwood Lane
14. Kingsley Place

15. Highgate Spinney
16. Hornsey Library
17. Broadwater Farm Estate
18. The Red House
19. Garton House
20. Wood Green Shopping City
21. Tile Kiln Studios

HARINGEY

Haringey, created from the Municipal Boroughs of Tottenham, Hornsey and Wood Green, is a borough of two halves; the rich, leafy uplands of Highgate and Muswell Hill and the poorer, urban lowlands of Tottenham and Wood Green. Correspondingly it has a mix of architectural styles and purposes; gleaming modernist homes and brutalist council blocks mix with bespoke artist studios and art deco factories. Most of the housing stock, and many other buildings, in the borough date from the Victorian and Edwardian eras, when the area developed after the expansion of the Great Northern Railway. There are plenty of interwar modernist buildings, including Berthold Lubetkin and Tecton's Highpoint I and II apartments in Highgate, one of the best examples of modernist architecture in Britain. Down the hill are the start of the Piccadilly Line-extension stations to Cockfosters, the beginning of Charles Holden and Frank Pick's modernisation of the underground network.

After the war, building continued in both the rich and poor parts of the borough. In Highgate and Muswell Hill, modernist houses and private estates appeared, like the Southwood Park estate by Douglas Stephen, or Walter Segal's experiment in self-building on North Hill. In areas like Wood Green and Tottenham, the 1960s and 1970s saw a big building programme, creating thousands of new council homes and facilities like libraries and community centres. The borough's architects' department was one of the most innovative in London, building a variety of housing types, including housing for single people and the disabled. Haringey architects' department designed housing estates such as Broadwater Farm and invited outside practices such as Colquhoun and Miller and Sheppard Robson to design other public buildings. As all across London these projects – homes, libraries, community centres – are under threat from both commercial and council-led redevelopment, such as the borough's recently thwarted Haringey Development Vehicle.

BARRATT CHOCOLATE FACTORY

1922–45

Joseph Emberton and P. J. Westwood

⊖ Wood Green N22 6UJ

George Barratt moved his confectionery business from Islington to Wood Green in 1880 and set up premises to expand his production. New factory buildings were constructed at

various stages between 1897 and 1953, with the most interesting modernist ones designed by Emberton and Westwood from 1922–45. On Coburg Road there is the 1922 building featuring a curved frontage, with a Dutch-inspired later building on Clarendon Road (now an artist's studio). In nearby roads there are also a number of mirror-glazed industrial units designed by Terry Farrell from 1979.

Modernist apartment blocks on North Hill in Highgate, designed by Berthold Lubetkin, originally for workers from Sigmund Gestetner's factory in Tottenham (also designed by Tecton, now demolished), but built for private tenants instead. Set on a sloping site, Highpoint I was built between 1933–5, and arranged in a double cruciform plan with each level having eight apartments, four large and four small. It was constructed of reinforced concrete, under the supervision of engineer Ove Arup, and finished in brilliant white render. The second building was added from 1936–8, and because of vigorous protests against the first building from locals, was finished in tile and brick infill. The apartments in the second block are larger, with more bedrooms and a rooftop swimming pool. Lubetkin himself took the penthouse apartment in the second block, moving from the first.

HIGHPOINT I AND II

1933–38   Grade I

Berthold Lubetkin and Tecton

⊖ Highgate N6 4BA

TURNPIKE LANE STATION

1932   Grade II

Charles Holden

N15 3NX

WOOD GREEN STATION

1932   Grade II

Charles Holden

N22 8HQ

BOUNDS GREEN STATION

1932   Grade II

C. H. James

N11 2EU

Three stations built as part of the Piccadilly Line extension to Cockfosters. These buildings were intended not just as stations but also as civic hubs, allowing people to connect between transport networks easily, as well as providing shopping and even cultural amenities. Turnpike Lane has a sunken, square ticket hall and was designed with connecting bus station and tram stops (the tram service was stopped in 1938).

Wood Green is part of a parade, built between two existing nineteenth-century buildings, and has a curved brick frontage. The interior originally featured a gallery space, now a staff room. On the platforms, as

at each station, there are ventilation grilles, designed by Harold Stabler, depicting the history of each location. Bounds Green was designed by C. H. James, who gave the station an octagonal ticket hall, another variation on Holden's 'Sudbury Box' design. The eight-sided shape allows more light into the ticket hall than in other Holden stations. At the bottom of the escalators are bronze uplighters, originally found at all of the extension stations, but now mostly removed.

HORNSEY TOWN HALL

1935   Grade II*

R. H. Uren

⊖ Hornsey N8 9JJ

Former town hall building by New Zealand architect Reginald H. Uren, who won the competition to design it for the Municipal Borough of Hornsey. Heavily influenced by Dutch architect Willem Dudok and his town hall at Hilversum, this L-shaped building has

a tall rectangular tower and a small green area in front. It is constructed of warm-coloured brick and the exterior has decorative ironwork grilles and a stone carving by A. J. Ayres. When

the Borough of Haringey was formed in 1965, the town hall was vacated and the new council moved into the civic centre at Wood Green. Today, Hornsey Town Hall is due to be turned into an arts centre and hotel.

CHOLMELEY LODGE

1935   Grade II

Guy Morgan

 Highgate N6 5EN

A six-storey art deco block of flats sitting on top of Highgate Hill with views over London. The building contains fifty-four flats and a facade made up of three curving crescents. The architect Guy Morgan, also known for Florin Court in Charterhouse Square, used an array of materials: yellow brick, cast stone, steel windows and concrete balconies. They all combine to produce a perfect example of the 1930s mansion block, a contrast to its

contemporary, the Highpoint building, just around the corner.

MUSWELL HILL ODEON

1936   Grade II*

George Coles

 East Finchley N10 3HP

A cinema on Fortis Green Road designed for the Odeon chain by the prolific architect George Coles. Unlike most of Coles' other designs, the Muswell Hill Odeon takes a

pared-down approach. It has a curved frontage, clad in cream and black tiling, but without the usual art deco frills. This was partly down the opposition of the church across the street to having a cinema so close by. The interior was subsequently made to be lavish and luxurious in contrast to the more sombre facade. The cinema design is one of the only remaining interwar cinemas influenced by German Expressionism, and is still showing films as part of the Everyman chain.

STUDIO, DUKE'S HEAD YARD

1939   Grade II

Tayler and Green

⊖ Highgate N6 5JJ

A wonderful International Style studio house tucked away just off Highgate High Street. It was designed for Punch

cartoonist Roger Pettiward by the duo of Herbert Tayler and Robert Green, better known for their post-war work in Norfolk. The house is three storeys tall and built in rendered brick, which was painted red on three sides of the house and grey on the other. The house also has a spiral staircase fitted into a drum tower, a sun terrace and timber window frames.

HARINGEY CIVIC CENTRE

1958   Grade II

Sir John Brown, A. E. Henson and Partners

⊖ Wood Green N22 8LE

Civic centre originally built for Wood Green Borough Council, and home to Haringey post-1965. It was designed by Sir John Brown, A. E. Henson and Partners, having won a competition for its design. The scheme consists of council chambers, offices, meeting

halls and a library. Its design was influenced by Scandinavian modernism, in particular Arne Jacobsen's work in Denmark. The building is constructed of brick and Portland stone around a reinforced concrete frame, and has generous glazing throughout, looking

to give an openness not usually seen in previous town hall designs.

SOUTHWOOD HOUSE ESTATE

1962

Andrews, Emerson and Sherlock

N6 5SX

SOUTHWOOD PARK

1965

Douglas Stephen and Partners

N6 5SQ

99–109 SOUTHWOOD LANE

1966

Edward Samuel

N6 5TB

KINGSLEY PLACE

1967

Architects Co-Partnership

 all Highgate, N6 5EA

Just off the Archway Road is a collection of post-war luxury housing, much of which is built on the site of the former Southwood House. The Southwood House Estate is a collection of various designs by Andrews, Emerson and Sherlock. Forty-three houses are arranged over the sloping, triangular site, all between two and three

storeys and three and four bedrooms, with pink brick, exposed concrete floor bands and sloping monopitch roofs. The Southwood Park Estate by Douglas Stephen and Partners has six linked apartment blocks of two and three-bed and studio flats, all with southerly facing living rooms.

On Southwood Lane are six terraced townhouses designed and built by Edward Samuel on the site of the old Hornsey Town Hall. Samuel and his wife Stella had previously built a modernist bungalow on the site but decided this row of townhouses would make more financial sense. Just off Southwood Lane is Kingsley Place, a collection of houses by the Architects Co-Partnership. The development features four different housing types, in one, two and three storeys, built in yellow brick and with horizontal concrete floor bands.

HIGHGATE SPINNEY

1966

John Howard and Bruce Rotherham

 Highgate N8 8AR

A five-storey apartment block consisting of thirty maisonettes near the centre of Crouch End. The building was constructed on the site of former Victorian houses, and designed to be in keeping with the terraces that

surround them, shown in the strong linear design of the block, which is constructed in red brick around a concrete frame. The apartments are a mix of studio and two-bed, with access from an external walkway at the rear.

HORNSEY LIBRARY

1965   Grade II

F. Ley and G. F. S. Jarvis

 Hornsey N8 9JA

Library building right next to the former Hornsey Town Hall with a variety of interesting features. The interior is spacious and light, featuring a glazed staircase window with an engraved map of Hornsey by Frederick J. Mitchell. The building also has a central courtyard with curtain wall glazing, a pool and concrete seating. On the exterior there is a curved brick façade above the entrance, coloured mosaic panelling and a bronze sculpture by T. E. Huxley-Jones set in a water feature. This building, the last by Hornsey

Municipal Borough before becoming Haringey, is a great example of the imagination and ambition of local authorities in the post-war era, sadly one not matched today.

BROADWATER FARM ESTATE

1967–71

C.E. Jacob and Alan Weitzel

⊖ Turnpike Lane N17 6NG

Although not as feted as neighbours Camden, Haringey's architects' department produced a range of buildings, from housing to libraries. The borough's flagship project was the Broadwater Farm Estate in Tottenham. Overseen by chief architect C. E. Jacob and deputy Alan Weitzel, the estate consists of twelve buildings connected by walkways, in a mix of high and low rise designed to house between 3,000–4,000 people. The architectural centrepieces are Tangmere, a six-storey ziggurat, combining shops and homes, with angled balconies, and the curved Boiler House. Following the riots of 1985, a regeneration plan was implemented, and over the next thirty years the estate was refurbished, leading to it having some of the lowest urban crime rates in the world and a lengthy waiting list to move onto the estate. At the time of writing, a question hangs over some of the buildings on the estate in the wake of the Grenfell tragedy.

THE RED HOUSE

1976

⊖ Hornsey N15 3PJ

GARTON HOUSE, ARCHWAY

1980

⊖ Crouch Hill N6 5XB

both Colquhoun and Miller

The duo of Alan Colquhoun and John Miller produced a number of projects for London boroughs between 1961 and 1988, including these buildings for Haringey. The Red House is a residential care home situated on West Green Road, containing accommodation for forty people and common rooms, kitchens and offices. The building is arranged on an awkward triangular site and constructed of orange-red brick. On Hornsey Lane is Garton House, a nine-storey apartment block with thirty-four flats for single people. It has a reinforced concrete frame faced with red brick and glass blocks. Colquhoun and Miller also designed a couple of steel Mies van der Rohe-inspired community centres for Haringey, one at Welbourne Road [demolished] and one on Whitehall Street.

WOOD GREEN SHOPPING CITY

1976–81

Sheppard Robson and Partners

PAGE HIGH

1976

Dry Halasz Dixon

 both Wood Green N22 6YQ

Megastructure in red brick and concrete, containing shops, offices, housing and parking on Wood Green High Street. Built as part of the Wood Green redevelopment which took place from the mid-1960s after the creation of the Borough of Haringey, by the time it was completed public opinion and economic pressures had made it into a relic of an earlier age. The residential section of the scheme is the Page High development by Dry Halasz Dixon, with housing arranged to form a 'street in the sky'. On the north side of Shopping City is Wood

Green Library (1978) by Bertram Dinnage of Haringey Borough Council, a stepped-back design that has recently been refurbished.

TILE KILN STUDIOS

1980

Peter Beaven

 Archway N6 5XH

An interesting group of studio houses sitting together just off the Archway Road. They were designed by New Zealand architect Peter Beaven, and are constructed of concrete blockwork painted white to give them a modernist air. These are no identikit boxes however, with differing heights, multiple sloping roofs and gable windows adding individuality to each house. The houses were built as part of a co-operative scheme, with the householders finishing the interior of the properties themselves.

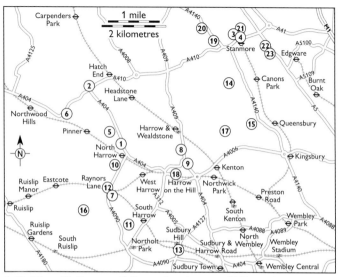

1. Clock Tower, Wealdstone Motors
2. Altham House
3. 2–10 Valencia Road
4. 1–6 Kerry Avenue
5. Capel Gardens and Pinner Court
6. Elm Park Court
7. Rayners Lane Grosvenor
8. Harrow Cannon
9. Harrow Granada
10. St Alban
11. St Paul's Parish Church
12. Rayners Lane Station
13. Sudbury Hill Station
14. Stanburn School
15. Kenmore Park Middle School
16. Roxbourne Infant and Junior Schools
17. Kenton Library
18. Harrow-on-the-Hill Station
19. 1 and 2 Halsbury Close
20. 1 and 3 Aymler Close
21. 14 and 16 Kerry Avenue
22. Stonegrove Gardens
23. 36 and 38 Lake View

HARROW

Like its neighbour Brent, Harrow features a wealth of interwar modernist designs, and not as much worth seeing from the post-war period. The borough has a variety of housing, with private houses, small estates and apartment blocks all represented. The best collection of houses is on the former Warren Estate in Stanmore, with contrasting groups of houses by Gerald Lacoste and Douglas Wood Architects. Further west in Pinner are two art deco apartment blocks, Capel Gardens and Elm Park Court, both built in anticipation of the suburbs becoming a mini-Hollywood. Staying with the silver screen, Harrow has a number of art deco cinemas, most prominently the former Rayners Lane Grosvenor, now a religious centre, designed by local architect F. E. Bromige. Bromige also designed the Harrow Cannon, equally as exuberant in design as the cinema at Rayners Lane, but now sadly covered in metal cladding.

Harrow also features a couple of modernist interwar churches just a short walk from each other, the Scandinavian-influenced St Alban by A. W. Kenyon and the equally austere St Paul's Parish Church by N. F. Cachemaille-Day. Work by the influential W. I. Curtis and H. W. Burchett for Middlesex County Council abounds in the borough. The pair oversaw the building of schools, clinics and hospital all over the now-disappeared county, with Stanburn School in Stanmore and Kenton Library being among their best work. Post war, the most interesting buildings are the private houses around Stanmore, with two Gerd Kaufmann designs in particular, 16 Kerry Avenue and 3 Aylmer Close, the highlights. As in Brent, post-war public housing is disappointing, with a couple of better efforts by Howell Killick Partridge Amis at Stanmore and borough architect G. J. Foxley in Pinner.

CLOCK TOWER, WEALDSTONE MOTORS

1933

🚇 North Harrow HA2 6EH

Art deco clock tower built as part of a parade of shops and flats. The car was a potent symbol of status in the interwar period, with more and more middle-class families investing in one. This led to an increase in car showrooms away from the traditional areas like Piccadilly and Great Portland Street in Central London. Showrooms such as this, designed in the latest architectural fashion, sprang up in the suburbs and around the newly built ring roads.

ALTHAM HOUSE

1934

W. J. Flower

🚇 Hatch End HA5 4RQ

Flat-roofed, white-walled house on a quiet suburban street in Hatch End, seemingly built and designed by W. J. Flower for himself. This house is a good example of the individually built moderne-inspired suburban home, not built by a famous architect or as part of a speculative development, but just as a family home in the contemporary fashion. It has all the design hallmarks of suburban art deco houses, including whitewashed walls, a central staircase tower and a curved doorway entrance.

2–10 VALENCIA ROAD

1935

Douglas Wood Architects

Stanmore HA7 4JH

Built on the former Warren Estate in Stanmore, these speculative houses were designed by Douglas Wood Architects. Nos. 2–10 were designed by the firm in the International Style with plain rendered walls, staircase towers and sun decks. The houses have an obvious vertical emphasis, with the staircase towers, vertical window strips and sun decks adding the

bulk of the buildings, already emphasised by their position on a slope. The large windows and sun decks came from the growing awareness and fashionability of the health benefits of sunlight and sun bathing.

1–6 KERRY AVENUE

1936

Gerald Lacoste

Stanmore HA7 4NJ

On a road intersecting with Valencia Avenue are six houses designed by Gerald Lacoste. Originally planned to be part of a larger modernist estate, these six were the only ones built. His six houses share many similar features with the Valencia Road buildings – flat roofs, rounded staircase towers, white walls – but are more circumspect in appearance. The houses are designed to be similar as a group but not monotonous, using the same elements in differing arrangements. Like the Douglas Wood houses, the Kerry Avenue buildings are constructed of brick, but have a mixture of exposed brick and rendered finishes. These houses were completed in 1937, and are now part of a conservation area along with the Valencia Road houses.

for those involved with the British film industry between the wars [see also Ealing Village p. 41]. Architecturally they consist of the same neo-colonial elements: white rendered walls, hipped roofs in green pantiles, steel Crittall windows (also in green) and landscaped grounds.

RAYNERS LANE GROSVENOR

1936   Grade II*

F. E. Bromige

⊖ Rayners Lane HA2 9TL

Exuberant art deco cinema designed by local architect Frederick Ernest Bromige, who specialised in designing cinemas. The front facade has a concrete mullion that is supposed to resemble an elephant's trunk. Inside, the building features a sunken tea room in the entrance and an auditorium with a proscenium arch. After closing as a cinema the building became a bar/disco and slipped into a state of disrepair. It was then bought as a centre for the Zoroastrian religion and extensively repaired and refurbished.

CAPEL GARDENS AND PINNER COURT

1936   Grade II

H. J. Mark

⊖ North Harrow HA5 5RG

ELM PARK COURT

1936   Grade II

H. V. Webb

⊖ Pinner HA5 3LH

Two lavish art deco apartment complexes built as prospective homes

HARROW CANNON

1936

F. E. Bromige

HA1 2TU

HARROW GRANADA

1937   Grade II

J. Owen Bond

HA1 2JN

 both Harrow on the Hill

Two cinemas in central Harrow, with differing levels of preservation. The Harrow Cannon is also by F. E. Bromige, with an equally spectacular art deco frontage. Unfortunately it has been hidden since 1962 under metal cladding, supposedly for safety reasons. It can only be imagined what state the design is in these days. The building is still operating as a cinema, screening predominantly Bollywood films, but developers are circling.

The former Harrow Granada was opened in 1937 and served as a cinema until 1996, before becoming a gym. It was designed for the Granada Theatres chain by J. Owen Bond with interiors by renowned designer Theodore Komisarjevsky. The exterior is designed in a rather plain modernist style, with the creativity saved for inside. Komisarjevsky included three decorative grilles either side of a proscenium arch, and chandeliers hung from the ceiling.

ST ALBAN

1937   Grade II

A. W. Kenyon

 North Harrow HA2 7PF

Scandinavian-influenced church in North Harrow; built in brown brick, with a square tower and shorn of much in the way of decoration. It was designed by A. W. Kenyon, who worked with Louis de Soissons at Welwyn Garden City, but this design is more radical than anything he produced in Hertfordshire. The structure is supported by reinforced concrete

ribs, around which brown Dutch bricks are arranged. The interior is as sparse as the exterior, with a finish of rough textured plaster.

ST PAUL'S PARISH CHURCH

1937   Grade II

N. F. Cachemaille-Day

 South Harrow HA2 8EL

Another quietly radical church design, located in a quiet road in South Harrow. This one was designed by N. F. Cachemaille-Day, sometime partner of Welch and Lander, but better known for his solo church designs throughout the country. This church is also built in brick, but rendered on the outside to resemble an austere factory building. Internally, decoration is eschewed, although it does feature some abstract stained glass designs from Christopher Webb.

RAYNERS LANE STATION

1938   Grade II

R. H. Uren and Charles Holden

HA5 5EG

76

SUDBURY HILL STATION

1933   Grade II

Charles Holden

HA1 3RA

Underground station designed by Reginald Uren and opened in 1938, five years after the Piccadilly Line was extended here. It was built as part of the New Works Programme, which saw the reconstruction of many underground stations and their works. The station was built to serve Harrow Garden Village, a housing development of the early 1930s that greatly increased the population of the area, necessitating a bigger station. Uren's original design was altered by Charles Holden, bringing it further into the street and allowing easier access to

STANBURN SCHOOL

1938

Canons Park HA/ ∠PJ

KENMORE PARK MIDDLE SCHOOL

1938

Queensbury HA3 9JA

ROXBOURNE INFANT AND JUNIOR SCHOOLS

1938

Rayners Lane HA2 9QF

all Curtis and Burchett

and from the station. The building itself is a typical box design with curved shopfronts. Sudbury Hill takes after its bigger brother Sudbury Town [*see Brent pp. 26–8*], with the addition of a couple of small shops either side.

W. T. Curtis and H. W. Burchett were respectively the chief architect and assistant architect for Middlesex County Council in the interwar years. In this period they built a range of buildings throughout the county,

including schools, libraries and health clinics. Schools were their most common design – they built hundreds between 1930 and 1946. These three schools in the Borough of Harrow are good examples of their aesthetic. Heavily influenced by Dutch architect Willem Dudok, the common elements in the buildings are the staircase tower, long, low flat roofs and wide window spaces. Of these three schools, Kenmore Park slightly breaks with the design rules by introducing a curved staircase tower.

KENTON LIBRARY

1939   Grade II

Curtis and Burchett

 Kenton HA3 8UJ

Another Curtis and Burchett design, this time for a library in the Harrow neighbourhood of Kenton. The trademark Middlesex County Council design elements are all there,

including the central staircase tower and low flat roof. The building was arranged in an L shape, with the adults' reading area on one side and the children's area on the other. This building is a great example of the interwar suburban library, something which along with its post-war counterpart has become increasingly rare as councils sell off assets to balance the books.

HARROW-ON-THE-HILL STATION

1939

Stanley Heaps

HA1 1BB

Metropolitan Line station built to serve Harrow-on-the Hill despite the protests of the famous private school who didn't want their pupils sullied by the spreading transport system. The station itself is an interesting design in brick, with the typical gullwing

platform canopies of the period. It was designed by Stanley Heaps, who was London Underground's chief architect from 1908 until 1945, although he was greatly overshadowed in this period by Charles Holden. Unfortunately it is hard to really appreciate Heaps' designs here due to the encroaching buildings on all sides of the station.

I AND 2 HALSBURY CLOSE

1939   Grade II

Rudolf Frankel

🚇 Stanmore HA7 3DY

Nos. 1 and 2 Halsbury Close were designed by émigré architect Rudolf Fränkel, who fled to Britain from Germany via Romania in 1933. No. 1, built in 1938 for Fränkel's sister, is made up of two brick cubes, one for a garage and one for the main house. The house features a cut-away corner that opens out onto the garden. No. 2, built for himself in 1938, is a simple box form finished in render and with tile hanging on the second floor. It was apparently altered in the 1970s to fit in with the new houses built behind it. Frankel mainly produced industrial

buildings in Britain, designing factories in London and Cheshire before moving to America in 1950.

I AYMLER CLOSE

1963   Grade II

Edward Samuel

3 AYMLER CLOSE

1968

Gerd Kaufmann

🚇 both Stanmore HA7 3EQ

This close on the private Aylmer Road estate features a couple of notable post-war houses. No. 1, designed by Edward Samuel in 1963, is a long low bungalow, built of brick and wood. Samuel, who trained under Basil Spence, was known for his bungalow designs, as well as his work on the townscape in Highgate. No. 3 is a brutalist-style concrete house, designed by Gerd Kaufmann, who also designed No. 16 Kerry Avenue, in 1967, and it echoes in its design the 1930s houses of Kerry Avenue and Valencia Road, with its circular staircase tower and flat roof.

14 KERRY AVENUE

1937

R. H. Uren

16 KERRY AVENUE

1968

Gerd Kaufmann

 both Stanmore HA7 4NN

STONEGROVE GARDENS

1968

HKPA

HA8 7TF

36 AND 38 LAKE VIEW

1960

HKPA

 both Stanmore HA8 7RU

At the northern end of Kerry Avenue in Stanmore are two individual modernist houses built thirty years apart. No. 14 was designed by Reginald Uren for himself and built in yellow brick in the International Style similar to the other houses in the area. Uren was a New Zealand-born architect who moved to Britain in 1930. His big break was his winning design for Hornsey Town Hall in 1933 [*see Haringey pp. 63–4*]. No. 16 is a much later building, designed and built in 1968 by the architect Gerd Kaufmann. It is constructed of brick, with large windows to create differing light levels in each room.

Stonegrove Gardens is a small housing scheme designed for Harrow Borough by the firm of Howell Killick Partridge and Amis. The scheme consists of one, two and three-storey brick houses built around an existing landscape of ponds and mature trees, and a small community centre in the grounds. The design creates the feel of a small village, slightly at odds with the municipal housing designs of its time. A short walk away are two private semi-detached houses by

HKPA in Lake View. The houses are timber framed with front balconies, resembling something you might find halfway up a mountain in Switzerland rather than the suburbs of London.

81

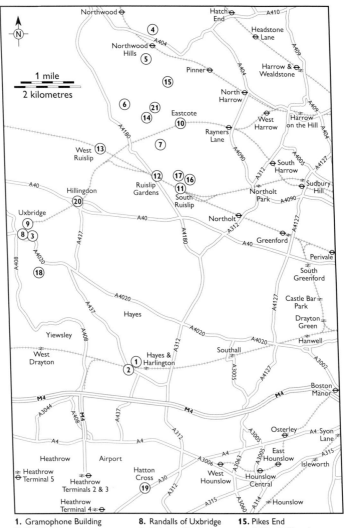

1. Gramophone Building
2. EMI Buildings
3. Uxbridge Regal
4. Northwood Way
5. Norwich Road and Joel Street
6. 97–101 Park Avenue
7. Lady Bankes School
8. Randalls of Uxbridge
9. Uxbridge Station
10. Eastcote Station
11. South Ruislip Station
12. Ruislip Gardens Station
13. West Ruislip Station
14. 152 Eastcote Road
15. Pikes End
16. St Mary's Church
17. St Gregory's Church
18. Brunel University Campus
19. Hatton Cross Station
20. Hillingdon Station
21. Highgrove Estate

HILLINGDON

The Borough of Hillingdon has some of the best and most varied modernist architecture in this book. From pioneering factories built in the early twentieth century to equally innovative housing built by the borough architects' department in the 1970s, the full gamut of modernist design can be explored here. As with many of the western London boroughs, the south of Hillingdon is the more industrial end, with the north being more suburban. Hayes in particular was a big industrial centre in the first half of the twentieth century, and boasts factories by Owen Williams and Wallis Gilbert and Partners. The northerly villages of Eastcote, Northwood and Ruislip became synonymous with suburbia and Metro-Land after the great housing estates were built in the 1920s and 1930s, and here we find some of the best modernist design such as Connell, Ward and Lucas' houses in Ruislip and one of Curtis and Burchett's best schools for Middlesex, Lady Bankes.

After World War II, Hillingdon underwent much change. One catalyst for this was the expansion of Heathrow from the small aerodrome of 1929 to one of the busiest airports in the world. This expansion did engender some modernist buildings; the main airport expansion was undertaken by Frederick Gibberd, with additional buildings designed by Yorke, Rosenberg and Mardall and Manning and Clamp. Hillingdon's post-1965 architects' department proved influential in its rejection of the high-rise concrete municipal orthodoxy in favour of a neo-vernacular style that encouraged pitched roofs and brickwork. Its flagship building was the borough council's own civic centre in Uxbridge, opened in 1977 and designed by RMJM. The building was unlike any civic centre building in the post-war period, replacing concrete uniformity with red brick, pitched roofs and an irregular frontage. Internally the usual warren of small offices were replaced by open-plan spaces arranged in four quadrants. The architects' department themselves, under the leadership of Thurston Williams, produced a range of innovative housing to accommodate single people, the elderly and the disabled.

GRAMOPHONE BUILDING

1912   Grade II

A. C. Blomfield and Owen Williams

UB3 1DD

EMI BUILDINGS

1929

Wallis, Gilbert and Partners

UB3 1HA

⊖ both Hayes & Harlington

Two factories built at the start of the twentieth century to serve the growing music industry. The Gramophone Building is the first known building by Owen Williams. It is a functional, six-storey building, with none of the adornments of most factories of its era, and looks forward to the modernist factory of the 1920s and 1930s, and across to the pioneering European factories of Behrens and Gropius. Next door is a set of buildings designed by Wallis, Gilbert and Partners, also for the Gramophone

Company (who became EMI in 1930). The site contained all the sections of the record production chain: manufacture, research, packing, administration and shipping. The style employed here by Wallis Gilbert & Partners was more pared down than their Great West Road buildings, with long brick ranges in white render. The complex has now been redeveloped with housing, shopping and leisure facilities. Nearby is the Hayes Cocoa factory of 1932, another Wallis Gilbert & Partners building.

UXBRIDGE REGAL

1931   Grade II*

E. Norman Bailey

⊖ Uxbridge UB8 1LD

Restrained art deco cinema in Uxbridge town centre by architect Eric Norman Bailey. The design has touches of Egyptian and Chinese

influences in its decoration, including a Chinese half-moon proscenium opening. The cinema closed in 1977, and the building has been a nightclub since 1984.

NORTHWOOD WAY

1934

Morgan and Edwards

HA6 1RB

NORWICH ROAD AND JOEL STREET

1934

Robert de Bugh

HA6 1ND

 both Northwood Hills

Two groups of moderne-style houses in the commuter village of Northwood Hills. The houses in Norwich Road and Joel Street were built by Modern Houses Ltd as part of the Joel Park Estate, capitalising on the opening of Northwood Hills station in 1933. Like the other speculative houses in Northwood Way, the houses here have elements of deco and modernism, attached to traditional house forms. Originally built with flat roofs complete with pergolas and sun decks, some now sport pitched roofs, but are generally well kept.

97–101 PARK AVENUE

1935   Grade II

Connell, Ward and Lucas

Ruislip Manor HA4 7UL

A contrast is presented to the Northwood houses with these three stark houses in Ruislip. Designed by Basil Ward of Connell, Ward and Lucas,

they were built as part of an envisioned larger estate of modernist houses. As often occurred with such plans in the interwar years, the general public's enthusiasm for flat roofs and white walls did not match the designers'. The finished houses consist of semi-detached pair and a single house. They are rectangular in form, constructed in concrete and feature sun patios. As with a few other Connell, Ward and Lucas houses, a long planning battle ensued between architects and the local council. Luckily for us, the architects won. A twenty-first century lookalike has been built at No. 103.

LADY BANKES SCHOOL

1936   Grade II

Curtis and Burchett

 Ruislip Manor HA4 9SF

Probably the best of Curtis and Burchett's many schools for the Middlesex County Council. The school has a long frontage in orange and beige brick, concrete lintels and the regulation staircase tower. The building is set in a rectangular plan with a central courtyard area. Next door is a nursery school, formerly a library and medical clinic, also by Curtis and Burchett and Grade II listed, added in 1939.

RANDALLS OF UXBRIDGE

1938   Grade II

W. L. Eves

 Uxbridge UB8 1QE

Elegant former furniture store in Uxbridge, rebuilt in the late 1930s and featuring some lovely period design features. The exterior has a square tower with flagstaff, a neon name sign and is finished in cream faience. The interior was plainer in style, and featured a pneumatic tube cash system.

EASTCOTE STATION

1939   Grade II

Charles Holden

HA5 1QZ

The store closed in 2015, and is being converted to apartments.

UXBRIDGE STATION

1938   Grade II

Charles Holden and L. H. Bucknell

UB8 1JZ

A pair of underground stations that show the decline in Charles Holden's inspiration in the late 1930s. Uxbridge is a building of two halves. The exterior presents a curving brick facade with abstract sculptures by Joseph Armitage; all rather fussy compared to earlier stations' forceful yet simple frontages. Inside, a totally different building. Taking Cockfosters as its inspiration, with portal frames in board marked concrete, Uxbridge looks towards the brutalist post-war style, as well as featuring stained glass panels by Ervin Bossányi. Eastcote is much simpler; a box-style ticket hall with curved shopfronts at street level. Perfectly in keeping with the style of earlier stations, but nothing revolutionary. In Holden's defence, he was at the time in the middle of designing his University of London project and had to rely on a number of collaborators

to help with the New Works station designs.

SOUTH RUISLIP STATION

1948–61

F. F. C. Curtis, John Kennett and Roy Turner

HA4 6TP

RUISLIP GARDENS STATION

1948

F. F. C. Curtis

HA4 6NF

WEST RUISLIP STATION

1948

F. F. C. Curtis, John Kennett and Roy Turner

HA4 7DW

Three stations built as part of the delayed Central Line extension to West Ruislip [see Ealing p. 88]. Unlike the Brian Lewis buildings, these stations were designed after World War II but beset by shortages and delays.

F. F. C. Curtis succeeded Lewis, and was responsible for the initial design of the three stations, with alterations made to his designs by John Kennett and Roy Turner. South Ruislip has a polygonal concrete-framed ticket hall with translucent glass panels, and a frieze in concrete by artist Henry Haig. Ruislip Gardens was supposed to have a raised Holdenesque ticket hall, but the finished design is a one-storey building with an exterior slate wall and an original roundel. West Ruislip does have a raised ticket hall in yellow and white concrete brick supported by a portal frame, with a splayed concrete front canopy.

152 EASTCOTE ROAD

1952

Dex Harrison

HA4 8DX

PIKES END

1968–70

Dore and Wurr

⊖ both Eastcote HA5 2EX

A couple of good examples of the early post-war suburban modernist aesthetic, marrying flat roofs with traditional materials like brick and timber. 152 Eastcote Road is a detached house with a monopitch roof and concrete floors, which are supported by thin steel columns, with walls of local yellow Uxbridge brick. Not far away [and actually in Harrow] is Pikes End, a collection of flat-roofed brick houses with tile hanging and timber on the outside. They were designed by Noel Dore and Peter Wurr, who built No. 1 for themselves, having lived in another house they designed for themselves nearby.

ST MARY'S CHURCH

1959

Lawrence King

HA4 0SP

ST GREGORY'S CHURCH

1967

Gerard Goalen

 both South Ruislip HA4 0EG

Two post-war churches showing the changes in church architecture from the end of World War II. St Mary's was designed in the 'festival' style, influenced by Scandinavian modernism. The church is constructed of yellow brick around a reinforced concrete frame, and has a folded concrete slab roof covered in copper, which was constructed with advice from Ove Arup and Partners. The large exterior crucifixion statue is by Brian Asquith, and there is stained glass work at the east end by Keith New. St Gregory's was designed by Gerard Goalen, and shows an interesting contrast with St Mary's; it is constructed of dark brick in an oval plan, which became fashionable in church design in the 1960s after the Second Vatican Council, allowing congregations to be much

closer to the altar. The interior features sculptures by Willi Soukup, and *dalle de verre* [slab in resin] glass by Dom Charles Norris, added in 1987–89, which can be seen either side of the doorway.

BRUNEL UNIVERSITY CAMPUS

1966–71   Grade II

Richard Sheppard Robson and Partners, Stillman and Eastwick-Field

 Uxbridge UB8 3PH

Brunel University underwent a major expansion in the 1960s, with a number of new buildings completed as part of a master plan by Richard Sheppard, most prominent of which was the lecture theatre. Designed by John Heywood of Richard Sheppard,

Robson and Partners, the structure is built from reinforced concrete, with projecting box-shaped lecture theatres, finished in board marked concrete. The lecture theatres are held up by concrete piers and a first floor of prefabricated concrete panels. Elsewhere on the campus are the library and chemistry buildings, also by Sheppard Robson, and the engineering block by Stillman and Eastwick-Field. The lecture theatre and other assorted campus buildings featured in Stanley Kubrick's film adaptation of *A Clockwork Orange*.

HATTON CROSS STATION

1975

London Transport Architects Department

TW6 3RE

HILLINGDON STATION

1987

Cassidy Taggart Partnership

UB10 9NR

These two tube stations show the ways post-war designers tried to incorporate, or reject, the influence of Charles Holden over station design. Hatton Cross is a 1970s version of a 'Sudbury Box', a large rectangular station in glass and cream tile, with a concrete frieze by William Mitchell running around the parapet. Hillingdon rejects the Holden box in favour of a deconstructed design in steel that bridges the tube line. Unfortunately both stations could well do with some upkeep.

HIGHGROVE ESTATE

1977

Edward Cullinan Architects

⊖ Ruislip Manor HA4 8EQ

An ingenious little estate of low-cost terraced houses designed for the Borough of Hillingdon by Edward Cullinan Architects, built in the former grounds of Highgrove House. The houses have wide frontages, with a flexible ground-floor living area, allowing the residents to divide space as they need. The houses originally had bright blue corrugated sloping roofs, but these have since been replaced. The houses are arranged in groups of four, with wide gardens and in-built garages.

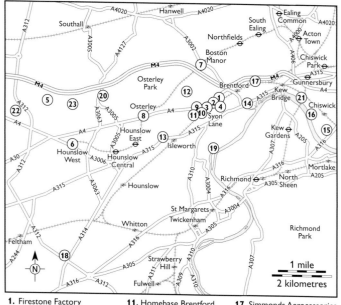

1. Firestone Factory
2. Pyrene Factory
3. Coty Cosmetics
4. Currys Factory
5. Hangar, Heston Aerodrome
6. Hounslow West Station
7. Boston Manor Station
8. Osterley Station
9. National Provincial Bank
10. Gillette Factory

11. Homebase Brentford
12. Pavilion and Clubhouse, Isleworth
13. Heston and Isleworth Fire Station
14. Brentford Health Centre
15. Polytechnic Stadium
16. University of London Boathouse

17. Simmonds Aerocessories
18. All Saints, Hanworth
19. All Saints, Isleworth
20. Wheatlands Estate
21. 23 Strand-on-the-Green
22. Holy Angels and St Christopher
23. Lovat Walk

HOUNSLOW

Much of Hounslow's modernist architecture is influenced by its rich industrial heritage. As part of Middlesex, what became Hounslow was quite rural in character, with much land bound up as part of the estates of country houses like Chiswick House, Osterley Park and Syon House. Brentford was the centre of trade in the area and when the Great West Road was built through the town, a section of it became known as the 'Golden Mile' due to its dazzling art deco factories, chiefly by Wallis, Gilbert and Partners. Sadly this area was not treated as the national treasure it should have been, and there has been much tarnishing of the Golden Mile, most notoriously in the sneaky demolition of the Firestone factory on August Bank Holiday weekend in 1980, before the building could be listed. Now all that remains of the factory are its gateposts.

Elsewhere in the borough there are a range of interesting and lesser-known modernist buildings. Aerodromes, stadiums, banks and health centres all feature a variety of interwar styles, from art deco to streamline modern to International Style modernism. Various post-war styles are represented as well; brutalism at the Penguin Warehouse at Harmondsworth, neo-vernacular by Edward Jones in Lovat Walk and high tech at Nicholas Grimshaw's Homebase on the Great West Road. Hounslow's own architects department largely used the widespread system-built concrete method to provide their construction needs. However, they did produce a few buildings of note, including the brutalist Heathlands School, with extra-thick concrete to protect it from aircraft noise, and the civic centre, with its landscape design by Preben Jakobsen, the latter now unfortunately demolished.

FIRESTONE FACTORY

1928   Grade II

PYRENE FACTORY

1930   Grade II

COTY COSMETICS

1932   Grade II

all Wallis, Gilbert and Partners

CURRYS FACTORY

1936   Grade II

F. E. Simpkins

 all Syon Lane TW8 9DN

A group of art deco factories along the Great Western Road outside Brentford, also known as the 'Golden Mile', mostly designed by Wallis, Gilbert and Partners. The first of these was the Firestone factory, built in 1928. Like many Wallis, Gilbert and Partners factories it consisted of an art deco main block fronting the road, with more functional production buildings behind. The design was a forerunner of the Hoover factory [*see Ealing pp. 39–40*] with rows of columns and corner staircase towers. Unfortunately all that remains of this building are the gateposts after it was disgracefully demolished in 1980.

However, a few other art deco factories still stand on this road. The Pyrene factory was built for a fire extinguisher manufacturer, directly opposite the Firestone site. It differs from the Firestone and Hoover buildings in having a square central tower of 110 feet, which contained the company design office, aided by available light from all sides including above. The building is constructed of white rendered brick around a steel frame. The Coty Cosmetics building, designed for a French perfume company, has a striking exterior of sculpted curves, quite different from Wallis, Gilbert and Partners' other buildings. Like all of the Golden Mile factories, it was designed with an art deco facade in front and a functional factory area behind. The factory area has now been demolished. Lastly, we have a non-Wallis Gilbert & Partners building, the former Currys factory by F. E. Simpkins. It is a lovely moderne-style building, with graceful curves and a small clock tower.

HANGAR, HESTON AERODROME

1929　Grade II

L. M. Austin and H. F. Murrel

 Hounslow West TW5 9PR

The first all-concrete aircraft hangar constructed in Britain, built as part of one of the earliest London airfields. It has a curved design made out of reinforced concrete, with a single eighteen-foot sliding door at the end facing the airfield. A control tower and clubhouse, also designed by the same architects, were demolished in the 1970s. The hangar is currently used as a warehouse.

HOUNSLOW WEST STATION

1931　Grade II

Charles Holden and Stanley Heaps

TW3 3DH

BOSTON MANOR STATION

1934　Grade II

Charles Holden

TW8 9LQ

OSTERLEY STATION

1934　Grade II

Charles Holden and Stanley Heaps

TW7 4PU

Another demonstration of the evolution of design between Charles Holden's first and second wave of stations for London Underground. Hounslow West is in the old style, a heptagonal ticket hall finished in Portland stone. Boston Manor and Osterley are more eye-catching and find Holden exploring different arrangements from the Sudbury Box. Boston Manor has a fin-style tower with glass bricks and a low station building. Osterley has a square brick tower topped with a concrete finial. These later stations show the influence of contemporary Dutch architecture on Holden, and serve as good examples of the station-as-advertisement idea beloved by Frank Pick.

NATIONAL PROVINCIAL BANK

1935　Grade II

W. F. C. Holden

GILLETTE FACTORY

1937   Grade II

Bannister Fletcher

HOMEBASE BRENTFORD

1988

Nicholas Grimshaw

 all Syon Lane TW7 5QE

Three more buildings on the Great West Road, just along from the art deco factories. Firstly, a branch of the National Provincial Bank by W. F. C. Holden, expressionist in style with its brick detailing and bowed front facade. Next door is the Gillette factory by Bannister Fletcher, with a 150-foot frontage, typical 1930s-style clock tower and windows with decorative metal aprons. It looks a bit sombre in comparison with the more exotic Wallis, Gilbert and Partners factories around the corner. Lastly a more contemporary building, a high tech-style superstore for Homebase by Nicholas Grimshaw. The entrance mast holds up a spine supporting seven curved spans which form the roof. This allows the interior to be column-free and gives a floor space of over 4,000 square metres.

PAVILION AND CLUB-HOUSE, ISLEWORTH

1935   Grade II

Sutcliffe and Farmer

 Syon Lane TW7 5DB

Stand built for University College School Old Boys Club by Brian Sutcliffe and H. C. Farmer with an exaggerated curved roof, giving it an almost expressionist air. The stand is constructed of reinforced concrete and features a refreshment room and amenities. It was completed in 1935 and used by the University Old Boys team until 1979, after which it fell into disrepair. The stand and clubhouse were listed in 2001 and the site was taken over and refurbished by a five-a-side football company in 2005.

HESTON AND ISLEWORTH FIRE STATION

1937

J. G. Carey

⊖ Isleworth TW7 4HR

Curving brick fire station situated at the junction of London and Spring Grove Roads, built to replace two separate stations. It was designed by J. G. Carey, borough surveyor, and the horizontal structure features twenty flats, as well as the engine house, offices, a recreation room and workshops. The style is influenced by the Dutch municipal buildings of Willem

Dudok, as many public service buildings of the 1930s were.

BRENTFORD HEALTH CENTRE

1938   Grade II

L. A. Cooper and K. P. Goble

⊖ Brentford TW8 0NE

Another Dutch-inspired building by the architects for the then Municipal Borough of Chiswick and Brentford. This health centre features typical 1930s modernist details – a flat roof, projecting curves and a central

tower containing a caretaker's flat. It originally contained a Juvenile Employment Bureau, and the building is now part of a primary school. Opposite is the county court, built in 1963 and designed by C. G. Pinfold of the Ministry of Public Building and Works.

POLYTECHNIC STADIUM

1937   Grade II

Joseph Addison

W4 3UH

UNIVERSITY OF LONDON BOATHOUSE

1936　Grade II

Thompson and Walford

W4 3TU

⊖ both Chiswick

The Polytechnic Stadium was built for use by Regent Street Polytechnic and designed by the school's head of architecture, Joseph Addison. It is constructed of reinforced concrete, with a mixture of in-situ and precast sections. The roof of the stand is supported by a seventy-eight-foot-long beam, which rests on two octagonal pillars. The stand has two seating sections and also contains offices, changing rooms and reception rooms. The stand was Grade II listed in 2003 and is still used by the University of Westminster, the successor to the polytechnic. Further

up the same road is the University of London boathouse, typical 1930s nautical modern; reinforced concrete, flat roof and steel railings.

SIMMONDS AEROCESSORIES

1936–42　Grade II

*Wallis, Gilbert and Partners and
G. A. Warren*

⊖ Kew Bridge TW8 9BS

Originally designed as a factory for Simmonds Aerocessories, this building has changed hands many times over the years and is currently an apartment block. The building consists of a monumental eleven-storey tower with one and two-storey flanking buildings, which have circular entrance towers on two corners. The east wing was designed by G. A. Warren in 1936, with Wallis, Gilbert and Partners adding the tower and other buildings from 1937–42.

ALL SAINTS, HANWORTH

1952–7   Grade II

N. F. Cachemaille-Day

⊖ Feltham TW13 5EE

ALL SAINTS, ISLEWORTH

1967–70   Grade II

Michael Blee

⊖ Isleworth TW7 6BE

Two post-war churches, both called All Saints, with contrasting histories. The main part of the church in Hanworth is square in plan, allowing all of the congregation a clear view of the altar. The building is constructed in brick with a concrete frame, shown in two arches that cross above the nave. All Saints in Isleworth has a longer history, originally being built in the fourteenth century. A fire in 1943 destroyed most of the church, save the tower. Michael Blee designed the new church, balancing the ancient tower with bold new red brick walls and projecting metal fins.

WHEATLANDS ESTATE

1963

Edward Schoolheifer

⊖ Hounslow East TW5 0SW

Speculative estate in Heston, designed by Edward Schoolheifer for Ronald Lyon Estates. The estate features an eleven-storey apartment block, and a variety of four, three and two-bedroom houses, all designed in pale brick among lawns and communal gardens. The estate also features the winner of the *Woman's Journal* 'House of the Year' award for 1963, No. 2, which was designed with an angular roofline and an internal courtyard. Unfortunately it is looking a bit dilapidated these days. Next door is Heston Farm estate (1968–72) by Hounslow Borough, with two tower blocks and terraced houses in grey brick.

23 STRAND-ON-THE-GREEN

1966

Timothy Rendle

 Gunnersbury W4 3PH

A slim 1960s house slipped into a eighteenth-century terrace alongside the Thames at Chiswick. The house is constructed of concrete and glass, fitting into a twelve-foot, six-inch plot on the towpath. Inside it features underfloor heating and a spiral staircase, and has a concrete relief number 23 on the exterior.

HOLY ANGELS

1971

Norman Haines Design Partnership

ST CHRISTOPHER

1971

Gerard Goalen

 both Hounslow West TW5 9RG

Two contrasting churches built side-by-side in Cranford, right under the flight path of Heathrow Airport. The Catholic church, St Christopher, combines spaces for worship and social interaction under one roof, and is formed of three polygonal structures of austere grey brick. The Church of England Holy Angels forms quite a contrast, being constructed of brown brick and having a more lively, vertical emphasis thanks to its multiple strip windows.

LOVAT WALK

1977

Edward Jones

 Hounslow West TW5 9HP

Housing for the elderly, containing fourteen homes arranged around a south-facing courtyard, designed by Edward Jones for Hounslow Borough. It is quite different to most social

100

housing of its day, having an almost Mediterranean feel with its white-washed walls, wooden pergolas and porthole windows. The houses look like they could do with a bit more care and attention in the present day, however.

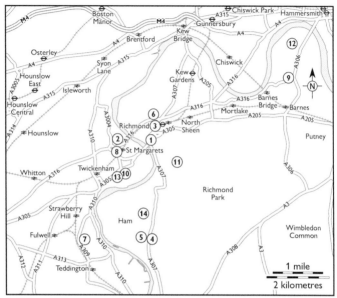

1. Richmond Odeon
2. 46 Ailsa Road
3. Richmond Station
4. Parkleys Estate
5. Langham House Close
6. Grandstand, Richmond Athletics Ground
7. Fieldend
8. St Margaret's
9. St Mary's Barnes
10. 25 Montpelier Row
11. Queen's Road Estate
12. Baynes House
13. 8c Orleans Road
14. 14 and 16 Arlington Road

RICHMOND

The Borough of Richmond upon Thames was formed from the municipal boroughs of Twickenham, Richmond and Barnes. Twickenham came from the county of Middlesex, with Richmond and Barnes joining from Surrey. Most of the borough is made up of parkland and residential areas, and so the architectural focus in Richmond is on the home. The neighbourhoods of Ham, Petersham, Twickenham and others have a wealth of modernist private houses, small-scale successors to the great country houses of the area like Hampton Court. The best-known modernist houses in the borough come from the post-war era, but there are pockets of deco-influenced houses in Twickenham and Fullwell. Spread around Ham Common is a wealth of housing from the 1950s and 1960s, including two contrasting icons of the age, the brutalist Langham House Close by Stirling and Gowan and the more serene Parkleys estate for Span Development by Eric Lyons. There are also a number of later one-off houses, showing how the changing architectural styles of the post-war period was reflected in the Englishman's castle.

Away from the residential, there are number of interesting modernist buildings in Richmond. The interwar period is represented by the art deco Richmond Odeon, positioned at one end of Richmond Bridge, and the more austere Richmond station, one of James Robb Scott's designs for Southern Railways. From the post-war period, there is the exposed concrete of the Richmond Athletic Grandstand, the brick Richmond Baths and the soon to be demolished magistrates' court by the Greater London Council. Like all the western suburbs, there are a number of post-war churches. The best of them is probably St Margaret's Twickenham by Williams and Winkley, along with the rebuild of St Mary's in Barnes by Edward Cullinan.

RICHMOND ODEON

1930   Grade II

Leathart and Grainger

 Richmond TW9 1TW

A cinema designed in what was known as the atmospheric style, with the emphasis on giving patrons a total experience through emulat-

ing designs from exotic countries or eras. This example in Richmond has a subdued frontage with three lion masks above the entrance. Inside, the appearance of a Spanish Moorish courtyard is given, with ornate grill-work, tiling, plaster decoration and hanging lanterns.

46 AILSA ROAD

1935

Couch and Coupland

 St Margarets TW1 1QW

A well-kept, Cubist-influenced house near the River Thames in Twickenham. The house is three storeys tall with a sunroof, and has a rectangular staircase tower. It is finished in brilliant white render and features a front door complete with jazzy motif. It was designed by the partnership of William Couch and William Coupland, who were based in the area, and designed many houses and apartment blocks in the 1930s.

RICHMOND STATION

1937

James Robb Scott

TW9 1EZ

Modernist-influenced railway station, designed by James Robb Scott, chief architect of Southern Railways. Scott oversaw the design and building of a number of stations for the newly formed Southern Railways from 1925 until 1939. Richmond station is built in

Portland stone, and features a roomy ticket hall and square clock above the entrance. The design suffers somewhat in comparison with the contemporary London Underground stations and from latter-day clutter, but is nevertheless an interesting example of the spreading modernist influence on 1930s British architecture.

the estate is spread around mature trees and hedges, allowing the estate to flow and be part of its neighbourhood. The buildings themselves are influenced by the Scandinavian modernism of the immediate post-war period, with flat roofs, timber windows and tile hanging predominant.

LANGHAM HOUSE CLOSE

1958   Grade II*

Stirling and Gowan

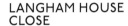 Richmond TW10 7JE

Thirty flats arranged in two and three-storey blocks, on a long thin plot behind Langham House off Ham Common. The scheme, designed by James Stirling and James Gowan, became a flag bearer for the 'New Brutalism' in the late 1950s. Reacting

PARKLEYS ESTATE, HAM COMMON

1956   Grade II

Eric Lyons

Richmond TW10 5LL

Span Developments was formed in 1956 by Geoffrey Townsend, and built over 2,000 speculative homes with Eric Lyons as the principal architect. One of their earliest and best estates is Parkleys, near Ham Common. Consisting of flats, maisonettes and shops,

against the fine detailing of the prevailing festival style, these flats have exposed concrete frames, stock brick infill and jutting drain gargoyles, influenced by the post-war work of Le Corbusier. Internally, the living spaces are planned around fireplaces in

exposed brick. They are only a short distance from the Parkleys Span estate but travelling in another direction in design terms.

GRANDSTAND, RICHMOND ATHLETICS GROUND

1958

Manning and Clamp

⊖ Richmond TW9 2SF

Athletics ground with a curved reinforced concrete grandstand, which replaced a previous timber stand. Designed by local partnership Manning and Clamp and engineered by Jenkins and Potter, the stand holds 1,000 spectators and features a Royal Box [for the Royal Horse Show], as well as offices and tea rooms. Opposite is a swimming pool on the edge of Old Deer Park, designed by Leslie Gooday and Partners and opened in 1966. The red brick building, which won a Civic Trust Award in 1967, is now Grade II listed.

FIELDEND, TWICKENHAM

1961

Eric Lyons

⊖ Strawberry Hill TW1 4TF

An interesting contrast to the Parkleys Estate, also by Eric Lyons. Unlike Parkleys, which feels like a continuation of its neighbourhood, Fieldend is arranged in its own separate space. The homes are also different, with fifty-one terraced houses in brick with weatherboarding. The houses come in two different types, T7 and T8, with the T7 type being slightly deeper.

Internally, both types are designed with an open plan arrangement and three bedrooms. Most of the properties have garages, which are separate to the house to keep traffic away from the communal grounds.

ST MARGARET'S

1968   Grade II

Williams and Winkley

⊖ St Margarets TW1 1RL

ST MARY'S BARNES

1984   Grade II*

Edward Cullinan

⊖ Hammersmith SW13 9HL

Richmond is well served by post-war churches, with two contrasting examples here. St Margaret's is built in white concrete block, and features a large social hall separated from the worship area by an electric sliding door. It incorporates the ideas of the New Churches Research Group, who aimed to bring clergy and worshipers closer together. St Mary's Barnes is the skilful rebuilding by Edward Cullinan of an ancient church gutted by fire in 1978. Cullinan added a new nave and crossing to the remaining fifteenth-century tower and medieval chancel. The most spectacular addition is the latticework timber ceiling in the new nave.

25 MONTPELIER ROW

1969   Grade II

Geoffrey Darke

⊖ St Margarets TW1 2NQ

Tall, thin brick house added onto a Georgian terrace by architect Geoffrey Darke of Darbourne and Darke, for himself. Despite the contrast in age with the older houses in the row, this modern interloper fits it in well due to its enterprising but sensitive design, with matching external materials and window spaces. Inside, the house's small footprint is

accommodated for by having split-level rooms. The interior is finished in exposed brick walls and pine wood-work.

QUEENS ROAD ESTATE, RICHMOND

1971–83   Grade II

Darbourne and Darke

 Richmond TW10 6JZ

Estate designed by Darbourne and Darke for the Richmond Parish Lands Charity, with the aim of keeping lower and middle-class families in the area. The design is a typical Darbourne and Darke scheme: a mix of houses and low-rise flats in red brick, all with gardens or roof terraces. Characteristic Darbourne and Darke details abound: ceramic street signs, glazed porches and communal exterior areas. The estate was built in three phases, with

the third phase [between Cambrian Road and Park Hill] completed by different architects; the contrast is stark.

BAYNES HOUSE, BARNES

1974

Noel and Alina Moffett

 Hammersmith SW13 9BX

Sitting on a suburban street in Barnes is Baynes House, sheltered housing that sprouts like concrete mushrooms

among the semi-detached houses. The building is formed of polygonal clusters, a typical Noel Moffett form, in red brick with concrete roof slabs. The clustered plan allows the residents privacy, while remaining part of a group, and creates courtyard garden areas. The Moffetts built similarly shaped retirement homes across London's suburbs, including Forman Court in Twickenham (1974).

8C ORLEANS ROAD

1985

Evans and Shalev

St Margarets TW1 3BJ

14 AND 16 ARLINGTON ROAD

1987–2001

David Chipperfield

Richmond TW10 7BY

Two later private houses demonstrating the revolving fashions of architectural style. The house on Orleans Road is by Eldred Evans and David Shalev, most well known for their Tate St Ives design, and is similar to its near neighbour, 25 Montpelier Road, in being squeezed into a tight plot on the end of an older terrace. The exterior is a simple postmodern cut-out, almost like a child's drawing of a house. Internally, a Z-shaped plan brings light in through three levels. The house in Arlington Road, designed for photographer Nick Knight and his family, shows the return of white-walled modernism in the 1990s, combining a house and studio in monolithic, rendered walls linked by a translucent fibreglass walkway. The house, which replaced a post-war brick home by Knight's father, looks out onto the rear garden.

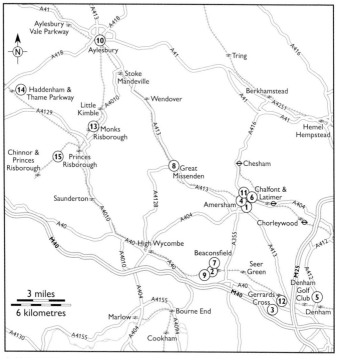

1. High and Over
2. Whitelands
3. Timbercombe
4. The Sun Houses
5. Denham Film Studios
6. Woodside Junior School
7. Beaconsfield Library
8. Great Missenden Library
9. Hampden Hill
10. County Hall
11. Community Centre
12. Marsham Lodge
13. Askett Green
14. Turn End
15. Lyde End

BUCKINGHAMSHIRE

The extended Metropolitan Railway left Hertfordshire and entered south-eastern Buckinghamshire, driving through Amersham and Great Missenden, pushing through Aylesbury before halting at isolated Verney Junction. The coming of the railway had the same effect here as in Middlesex and Hertfordshire; small villages and towns like Gerrards Cross grew in size as commuters flocked to live in the speculative estates built to entice them.

Architecturally the arts and crafts style was popular in Bucks, already home to houses by Edwin Lutyens and C. F. A. Voysey. However, a number of modernist and art deco houses were built in the interwar years. The most prolific designers were Collcutt and Hamp, who built many deco-influenced detached houses in the stockbroker towns of Beaconsfield and Gerrards Cross, most now demolished or altered. The more purely modernist International Style was also represented with houses by some of interwar architecture's bright young things. Amyas Connell (High and Over), Val Harding of Tecton (Egypt End) and Mendelsohn and Chermayeff (Shrubs Wood) all bought a taste of the Bauhaus to Bucks. Other interwar modernist buildings were few and far between, with the Denham Film Lab by Gropius and Fry and the various, now largely demolished, London Transport bus stations of Wallis, Gilbert and Partners being the exception.

Post war, as in Hertfordshire, modernism became the style of the welfare state. The county's architects department designed and built a large number of schools, fire stations, hospitals and other buildings, much of a very good quality. The majority of this work was carried under the leadership of Fred Pooley, who used the system-building method to provide the county with the services its booming population needed. Of course the biggest area of post-war building came in the new town of Milton Keynes, but as with Hertfordshire's new towns, we will leave that to another guide. We should also note the work of architect Peter Aldington and the array of houses he designed in the county – most notably Turn End at Haddenham, built for himself, a mixture of modernism and vernacular, with wonderful landscaped gardens.

HIGH AND OVER

1929   Grade II*

Amyas Connell

⊖ Amersham HP7 0BP

Designed by Amyas Connell, and completed in 1929, this house was one of the first modernist houses in the country and one of the most famous due to the publicity after it was built. Connell designed the house for Professor Bernard Ashmole, then Professor of Art and Archaeology at the University of London. The house is arranged in a Y plan, with three wings radiating from a hexagonal centre. The stark white walls, sun terrace areas and glazed staircase were all elements borrowed by Connell from contemporary European architecture, particularly Le Corbusier's early house designs. Despite the appearance of solid concrete walls, as with many early modernist houses in Britain, it is in fact white rendered brick around a concrete frame. The grounds contained a gardener's lodge, an electrical substation and a concrete water tower, as well as a sculpted modernist garden. Unfortunately the garden and water tower were demolished as the grounds were sold off for the 1960s housing estate that now surrounds this essential piece of modernism in metro-land.

WHITELANDS, BEACONSFIELD

1933   Grade II

Collcutt and Hamp

Beaconsfield HP9 1HL

TIMBERCOMBE, GERRARDS CROSS

1936

C. Mervyn White

Gerrards Cross SL9 7NW

In contrast to High and Over's high-minded International Style, here we have what might be called Stockbroker Moderne. Along the avenues of Gerrards Cross and Beaconsfield stand a number of modernist-influenced houses, white walls among the half-timber. Many of the houses have had pitched roofs added, but a few have kept their flat-roofed heritage. The best of them is Whitelands on Gregories Road, Beaconsfield. Designed by Stanley Hamp, it wears its modernism proudly, with a bold Cubist form enlivened by various vertical and horizontal Crittall windows.

THE SUN HOUSES, AMERSHAM

1935   Grade II

Connell and Ward

Amersham HP7 0BN

Four more modernist houses on the same hill as High and Over. They were designed by Amyas Connell after he had gone into partnership with Basil Ward in 1933. The houses form a piece with their big brother further up the hill, with their cubic forms, white walls and sunroofs. Indeed they

were supposed to be part of a bigger estate of thirty houses, which unfortunately was not built. Unlike High and Over, these sun houses are built entirely of concrete.

DENHAM FILM STUDIOS

1936   Grade II

Walter Gropius and Maxwell Fry

▴ Denham UB9 5HQ

Former film studios on the outskirts of London, now converted to apartments, where films such as *Great Expectations* and *Brief Encounter* were made. Many of the studio buildings have been demolished, but the laboratory buildings by Walter Gropius and Maxwell Fry survive. Gropius, founder of the influential Bauhaus school, moved to England for three years and worked in partnership with Maxwell Fry. Their buildings here are typically International Style – white painted concrete with flat roofs and projecting balconies and canopies.

WOODSIDE JUNIOR SCHOOL, AMERSHAM

1957   Grade II

David and Mary Medd with Clive Wooster

▴ Amersham HP6 6NW

Junior school designed by David and Mary Medd, who previously worked for Herts County Council, alongside Clive Wooster for the Ministry of Education. The school is built with traditional materials like brick and wood, but in standard specification, thus cutting down on costs. Two sets of

four classrooms are separated by an internal courtyard, alongside a glazed entrance hall, dining room and assembly hall with a sloping roof. David Medd also designed the furniture and fittings to be child sized, and artworks by Dorothy Annan were included in the fabric of the building.

BEACONSFIELD LIBRARY

1957

F. B. Pooley

Beaconsfield HP9 2NJ

GREAT MISSENDEN LIBRARY

1970

Rowan Walker and Derek Turner

Great Missenden HP16 0AL

The single biggest architectural influence on the county in the post-war period was Fred Pooley, chief architect for Buckinghamshire from 1953 to 1974. His department designed and built a range of buildings – housing, law courts, fire stations and more. Here are two libraries showing his contextual style, known as 'rationalised traditional'. Beaconsfield Library is a simple, open space, now altered with an all-glass frontage but obviously still much loved by its users. Great Missenden is more dramatic with its steeply pitched roof and triangular shape, yet echoes the style of local barn buildings.

HAMPDEN HILL, BEACONSFIELD

1963

Mary Christian Hamp

Beaconsfield HP9 1BP

On the outskirts of Beaconsfield is a collection of intriguing post-war houses arranged around a green on a steep slope. The twenty-nine houses were designed by Mary Christian Hamp, daughter of Stanley, who designed many houses in the area. The houses are built in brick with steeply pitched, asymmetrical roofs, The buildings are tucked into the landscape, turning their back on the street and opening out towards the distant rolling hills. Inside the houses have a split plan, making the most of the spectacular views. The estate is now a conservation area.

A more boldly brutalist building than the usual Bucks County Council designs of its era, but still well detailed and balanced. Built as the new headquarters for the county council, the scheme entails a 200-foot tower block, with a library, records office and registry below. The tower block is quite slim, with offices in canted groups designed to draw natural light in. The granite cladding and mirrored windows make an interesting contrast, and give the tower an otherworldly glow at certain times of day.

COUNTY HALL, AYLESBURY

1966

F. B. Pooley and Malcolm Dean

 Aylesbury HP20 1UA

COMMUNITY CENTRE, AMERSHAM

1968

F. B. Pooley

 Amersham HP6 5AH

Flat-roofed community centre in brick built as part of the civic centre alongside the library (1961), with a police station (1961) and the law courts (1968) to the south. The community centre is largely single storey, with a double-height roof for the hall area, and has textured tiles on one exterior wall. The centre, as well as the other buildings, are typical designs by the county council under Pooley; small scale, approachable and well detailed. Modernism with a small 'm'.

of Eric Lyons' other work for Span; brick houses faced with tile hanging or board, open-plan interiors, mono-pitch roofs and spacious grounds. The development has twenty-five houses of the C30 design, only used at one other Span development, at Taplow, also in Bucks, The landscaping was designed by Danish landscape architect Preben Jakobsen, who worked extensively with Lyons after settling in Britain in 1961.

MARSHAM LODGE, GERRARDS CROSS

1969

Eric Lyons

 Gerrards Cross SL9 7AB

A small piece of Span in Buckinghamshire. This estate on the outskirts of Gerrards Cross has all the hallmarks

ASKETT GREEN

1961–3   Grade II

Peter Aldington

⊖ Monks Risborough HP27 9LR

TURN END, HADDENHAM

1963–8   Grade II*

Peter Aldington

⊖ Haddenham HP17 8BG

HOUSES, LYDE END, BLEDLOW

1973–80   Grade II

Aldington and Craig

⊖ Princes Risborough HP27 9PP

Peter Aldington, and his later partners John Craig and Paul Collinge, created a range of housing in Buckinghamshire and beyond, marrying traditional and modern, interior and exterior. The house at Askett reimagines the traditional cottage, with a long sloping roof and almost blank street-facing facade. The interior features an open-plan, double-height living space. At Haddenham are three single-storey houses (Turn End, Middle Turn and The Turn), each with its own courtyard. Peter and Margaret Aldington still live at Turn End, and the property is open on selected days throughout the year. The homes at Lyde End were designed for Lord Carrington, who wanted to build houses for local residents. They share many of the features of the house in Askett Green, including split pitch roofs, an almost blank street wall and a combination of brick and timber construction.

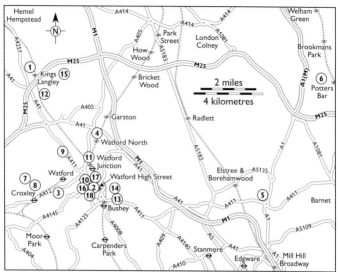

1. Ovaltine Court
2. Watford Essoldo Cinema
3. Sun Printers Clock Tower
4. Odhams Press
5. RNLI Centre
6. Library and Clinic
7. Little Green School
8. Malvern Way School
9. Sugden House
10. Telephone Exchange
11. Hille House
12. Gade View Gardens
13. 2 Grange Road
14. 4 Woodlands road
15. St Saviours
16. 60 Exchange Road
17. Car Park
18. Car Park

HERTFORDSHIRE

The Metropolitan Railway plunged into the western edge of Hertfordshire at Moor Park, taking in towns and villages like Rickmansworth and Chorleywood as well as the more built-up Watford. This led to an inevitable increase in population and house numbers. These days Watford is a de facto part of London, and the Metropolitan tube line has one terminus there. Architecturally modernism was resisted for longer in this part of Hertfordshire than the suburbs to the south, with only a few art deco houses or cinemas appearing before World War II, with the arts and crafts style holding sway with houses by C. F. A. Voysey in Chorleywood and Bushey.

Like the rest of the county, modernism came to the Three Rivers area in full effect in the post-war period. Architects and planners were tasked with building facilities for the massive population influx in and after the war years, mainly from London. In the east of Hertfordshire, this meant the founding of the new towns like Stevenage and Hemel Hempstead, successors to the garden cities of Letchworth and Welwyn. In the more built-up west, it meant the additions of some of post-war architecture's most famous names; Ernő Goldfinger, Alison and Peter Smithson and Yorke, Rosenberg and Mardall all designed buildings in the area.

The most famous contribution of Hertfordshire to post-war architecture was the output of the Herts County Council architects' department, first under C. H. Aslin and Stirrat Johnson-Marshall and then G. C. Fardell. The influx of school-age children led to a drastic lack of school buildings. Aslin, Johnson-Marshall and John Newsom, the county's chief education officer, reacted by adopting a prefab construction system for the schools, whilst also encouraging their young architects to adopt flexible interior spaces decorated with artworks commissioned from up-and-coming artists. They built 200 schools between 1945 and 1961, and their ideas spread throughout Britain and further abroad as architects left the department to work for London County Council and the Ministry of Education.

OVALTINE COURT

1923–9

J. A. Bowden

 Kings Langley WD4 8GY

Former factory for Ovaltine beside the Grand Union Canal at Kings Langley. A. Wander Ltd established a factory here in 1913 to increase production, with the premises expanding over the next twenty years. The art deco extension was designed by architect J. A. Bowden. Bowden also designed a model dairy farm for Ovaltine a little further east in 1932, based on a farm built by Louis XVI for Queen Marie Antoinette. Both the factory extension and the dairy farm have now been converted to housing.

WATFORD ESSOLDO CINEMA

1932

George Coles

 Watford High Street WD18 0GU

Art deco former cinema in central Watford designed by George Coles. This building replaced an earlier cinema, and bears some resemblance to Coles' design for the Gaumont Kilburn [*see Brent p. 30*] with its central tower and vertical emphasis. The interior was designed by Theodore Komisarjevsky and at its height, held nearly 1,300 cinema-goers. It only

lasted as a cinema until 1968 before becoming a bingo hall. It was recently converted into apartments and shops.

SUN PRINTERS CLOCK TOWER, WATFORD

1934

George W. Knight

Watford WD18 8AP

Printing was one of the chief industries in Watford in the first half of the twentieth century and its industrial architecture reflects this. This pump station and clock tower once

belonged to the large Sun Printers factory on Whippendell Road where the *Mail on Sunday* and *Sunday Times* were printed. The building is a curious hybrid between art deco and arts and crafts, with white rendered walls, green pantiled roof and SUN spelled out in geometric letters on the small tower. It is now awaiting a new purpose in life as the area has been redeveloped.

ODHAMS PRESS, WATFORD

1937–54

Owen Williams and Yates, Cook and Darbyshire

Watford North WD24 7RG

Sun Printers rival Odhams Press had their own modernist factory building on the other side of Watford, near Garston. The original 1937 printing hall was designed by Owen Williams in a functional style, a long low building of brick and with continuous windows and concrete lintels. The Press Hall building was added in 1954 by the firm of Yates, Cook and Darbyshire. They included a Scandinavian-influenced tower that includes art deco clock faces. The building has now been converted into offices and a supermarket. Another modernist factory in Watford associated with the printing trade was by Wallis, Gilbert and Partners for Ault and Wiborg, built opposite the Odhams complex, but demolished in 2007.

RNLI CENTRE, BOREHAMWOOD

1939

Kenchington and Farms

 Elstree and Borehamwood WD6 2BT

Building originally for the Royal National Lifeboat Institute on the Barnet Bypass at Borehamwood. Designed

by Herbert Kenchington in a moderne style, it contained offices, storerooms and workshops as well as cottages and an air raid shelter. It has a staircase tower with a lookout-style top floor. The building was originally brick, but has now been rendered. Nearby on the corner of Ripon Way was a now-demolished factory by Wallis, Gilbert and Partners for the John Laing building company, intended to be part of a larger Garden City.

LIBRARY AND CLINIC, POTTERS BAR

1939

Middlesex County Council

Potters Bar EN6 3AB

A slice of Middlesex modernism in Hertfordshire, this combined library and clinic was designed by the Middlesex architects' department,

led by W. T. Curtis and H. W. Burchett. Potters Bar was part of Middlesex until 1965, when it was transferred to Hertfordshire. The building follows in the Dudok-influenced style of Middlesex County Council found elsewhere in the book: brick construction, flat overhanging concrete roof and long thin windows. Middlesex often combined a library and clinic in this way, catering for both the mind and body.

LITTLE GREEN SCHOOL

1949

Herts County Council

WD3 3NJ

MALVERN WAY SCHOOL

1949

Herts County Council

WD3 3QQ

 both Croxley Green

Two Herts County Council schools in Croxley on the outskirts of Watford, designed by David and Mary Medd and opened on 6 May 1949. Both schools are well sited in spacious grounds, with the school buildings themselves being the most modest part of the scheme. As with other Herts schools of the era, they are constructed of prefabricated panels made to standard sizes. Inside the old-style rows of desks facing a blackboard was dispensed with in favour of space, light and exploration.

SUGDEN HOUSE, WATFORD

1956   Grade II

Alison and Peter Smithson

Watford Junction WD17 3DF

House designed for the engineer Derek Sugden of Arup Associates, who wanted a 'simple but radical' house. After Alison Smithson's initial design featuring a butterfly roof was rejected, the Smithsons produced a simplified design. The finished house features a catslide tile roof, an exterior of second-hand London brick around a reinforced concrete frame and thin steel-framed windows. The Sugdens' small budget meant the Smithsons used standard building materials arranged in way to make the house unique rather than using bespoke windows, beams, etc. This arrangement gives the house slightly curious air, an everyday house pulled apart and stuck back together again, and all the better for it.

TELEPHONE EXCHANGE, WATFORD

1956–68

Ministry of Works and Hubbard and Ford

 Watford Junction WD18 0GB

A building that shows the changes in modernist design in the post-war period. The first part of the Telephone Exchange building was designed by the Ministry of Works for the General Post Office in 1956 in a standard municipal modernist style; five storeys of sober brick and render, with some nice details in glass brick and yellow and orange tile. The extension by Hubbard and Ford, completed in 1968, is a different animal altogether. Aggressive, precast concrete panels form the structure, with a varied rhythm of windows. Not a satisfying whole but an interesting hybrid.

HILLE HOUSE, WATFORD

1959–61

Ernő Goldfinger

Watford Junction WD24 4AE

An office, showroom and factory complex on the St Albans Road, built on the site of an old Wells brewery. Hille House is an instantly recognisable Goldfinger building, constructed

with a reinforced concrete frame and an Uxbridge brick infill. It also features a central cantilevered box with coloured glass, a Goldfinger signature repeated at Alexander Fleming House and Trellick Tower. The Hille furniture company were patrons of modernist designers, with offices in Piccadilly by Peter Moro, and designers such as Robin Day and Fred Scott on their staff.

GADE VIEW GARDENS, ABBOTS LANGLEY

1961

Ernő Goldfinger

⊖ Kings Langley WD4 8PH

Just outside Watford, Goldfinger was commissioned by Watford Rural District Council to build a social housing estate. The originally planned nine-storey apartment block was rejected by the council, and a smaller scheme of terraced houses and small apartment blocks was built instead. As with much post-war social housing in the UK, the estate was allowed to deteriorate until it was unlivable, and demolished in 2012. However, a row of four terraced houses still survives, a remnant of Goldfinger's only social housing project outside London.

2 GRANGE ROAD

1933

Broad and Patey

WD23 2LE

4 WOODLANDS ROAD, BUSHEY

1962

John Prizeman

⊖ both Bushey WD23 2LR

Two contrasting modernist houses in an area noted for its arts and crafts houses, including one by C. F. A. Voysey. 2 Grange Road is deco-influenced house of 1933, constructed of rendered brick, with green brick banding horizontally across the first floor, as well as green steel window frames. Around the corner in Woodlands Road is Palafitte, a 1962 house designed by John Prizeman. The house is timber framed with the first floor supported by thin metal stilts, allowing space for car parking underneath, and a shallow butterfly roof. Prizeman was better known for his kitchen designs and his illustrations for architecture books.

ST SAVIOURS, ABBOTS LANGLEY

1963

John Rochford and Partners

⊖ Kings Langley WD5 0DS

Large Roman Catholic church in Abbots Langley which opened in 1963. It was designed by John Rochford and Partners, noted church designers from Sheffield. The church is constructed of concrete, with a red brick exterior and an aluminium and fibreglass mural by David John above the entrance. Inside the vaulted timber ceiling creates a spacious, single area decorated with a metal Stations of the Cross mural and more recent stained glass windows.

60 EXCHANGE ROAD, WATFORD

1964

H. E. Morgan for Richard Seifert

⊖ Watford Junction WD18 0JJ

Opposite the Telephone Exchange [*see above p. 126*] is this curved office building, originally built for H. J. Heinz, now a JobCentre. It was designed by H. E. Morgan, an architect with Richard

CAR PARKS, WATFORD

1965–70

B. L. Williams and F. C. Sage

⊖ Watford Junction WD17 2PS/
WD18 0PP

Seifert and Partners, the firm who did so much to transform the face of London and the suburbs with their flashy office blocks built on small, often bomb-damaged plots. This is slightly different from the normal Seifert block in being long rather than tall, and has a cantilevered floor at one end. Another modernist office block in same road by Douglas Stephen and Partners [1965] has now been demolished.

The centre of Watford underwent a transformation from the mid-1960s, with the town centre pedestrianised and a new shopping centre built. As part of this modernisation, a number of car parks were constructed. Designed by Williams and Sage of the borough engineers department, car parks in Rosslyn Road, Exchange Road and Estcourt Road all feature helix spiral ramps and rugged concrete construction. The car park in Exchange Road, opposite St Mary's Church, also has a patterned concrete wall.

References

BOOKS

Bettley, James, Bridget Cherry and Nikolaus Pevsner, *Buildings of England: Hertfordshire*, Yale University Press, London, 2019

Brandwood, Geoffrey K., Nikolaus Pevsner and Elizabeth Williamson, *Buildings of England: Buckinghamshire*, Penguin, London, 1994

Caddy Dennis G. J, *A Jewel for Metroland*, London Borough of Harrow, Harrow, 1983

Cantacuzino, Sherban, *Howell, Killick, Partridge and Amis: Architecture*, Lund Humphries, London, 1981

Cherry, Bridget and Nikolaus Pevsner, *Buildings of England: London 2: South*, Yale University Press, London, 1983

——, *Buildings of England: London 3: North West*, Yale University Press, London, 1991

——, *Buildings of England: London 4: North*, Yale University Press, London, 2002

Colquhoun, Alan and John Miller, *Colquhoun, Miller and Partners*, Rizzoli, New York, 1988

Cottam, David and David Yeomans, *Owen Williams: The Engineer's Contribution to Contemporary Architecture*, Telford, London, 2001

Edward Cullinan Architects, RIBA Publications, London, 1984

Elwall, Robert, *RIBA Drawing Monograph No. 3: Ernő Goldfinger*, Academy Editions in collaboration with the Royal Institute of British Architects, London, 1996.

Eyles, Allan and Keith Skone, *Cinemas of Hertfordshire*, University of Hertfordshire Press, Hatfield, 2002

Green, Oliver, *Metro-Land: British Empire Exhibition Number*, Oldcastle Books Ltd, Harpenden 2015

Jensen, Finn, *Modernist Semis and Terraces in England*, Ashgate, Farnham, 2012

Jones, Edward and Christopher Woodward, *A Guide to the Architecture of London*, Weidenfeld & Nicolson, London, 2013

McKean, Charles and Tom Jestico, *Guide to Modern Buildings in London: 1965–75*, Warehouse Publishing, London, 1976

Metro-Land: A Comprehensive Description of the Country Districts served by the Metropolitan Railway, Metropolitan Railways, London, 1924

Nairn, Ian, *Modern Buildings in London*, London Transport, London, 1964

——, *Nairn's London*, Penguin, Harmondsworth, 1988

Powers, Alan, *Aldington, Craig and Collinge: Twentieth Century Architects*, RIBA Publishing, London, 2009

Risselada, Max and Dirk van den Heuvel, *Alison and Peter Smithson: From the House of the Future to a House of Today*, 010 Publishers, Rotterdam, 2004

Sharp, Dennis and Sally Rendell, *Connell, Ward and Lucas: Modern Movement Architects in England 1929–39*, Frances Lincoln, London, 2008

Skinner, Joan, *Form and Fancy: Factories and Factory Buildings by Wallis, Gilbert & Partners, 1916–39*, Liverpool University Press, Liverpool, 1997

Webb, Michael, *Architecture in Britain Today*, Hamlyn for Country Life Books, Feltham, 1969

JOURNALS

For contemporary accounts of the buildings in this guide, you may consult the following journals at the Royal Institute of British Architects Library at 66 Portland Place, London:

The Architects' Journal
Architecture & Building News
The Architectural Review
Building
Twentieth Century Society Journal 13: The Architecture of Public Service

Acknowledgements

First of all, I would like to thank Charlie Mounter for initiating this project and making *A Guide to Modernism in Metro-Land* a reality. I would also like to thank all those at Unbound who helped with the project, in particular Georgia Odd, Mathew Clayton and Imogen Denny.

Obviously, I would like to thank all those who supported the book by making a pledge. I won't list all of your names as they are already listed elsewhere in the book. I really appreciate all of the extra publicity given to the project on social media and I would like to thank the following for their help: David Walker [@WowHauser], Tim Dunn [@MrTimDunn], Ian Visits [@ianvisits] and Diamond Geezer [@diamondgeezer].

Thanks also to all the various societies and organisations who helped the crowdfunding by including it on their sites and newsletters, these include Manchester Modernist Society, Cela Selley and the Twentieth Century Society, Michael Wright and Isokon Gallery, the Cinema Theatre Association, Foster + Partners, Manser Practice, the *Guardian*, the Archer, *Harrow Times*, *MyPinnerNews*, *Architecture Today*, the *Robert Elms* Show, The Modern House, Darran Anderson and *White Noise*, Feargus O'Sullivan and *CityLab*, Don Brown and the London Society, Enfield Society, Barnet Society, Finchley Society, Pinner Local History Society, Southgate Civic Trust, Rickmansworth Local History Society and Palmers Green Community. Apologies if I have missed any organisation or group out.

Thank you to James Bettley for answering all my questions on the buildings of Hertfordshire.

Thank you to Mike, Mum and Dad for your support before and during the project, both material and spiritual.

Thank you most of all to Lizzie and Benjamin, without whose patience, encouragement and love Modernism in Metro-Land and this guide book could not have happened.

A Note on the Author

Born in Reading, Joshua Abbott has lived in the US, Estonia and Mongolia, among other countries. Modernism in Metro-Land began as a university project at the University of Westminster; it now encompasses a website, guided tours and a book. He works as a photographic printer in Hoxton, and lives in Welwyn Garden City.

@MOD_IN_METRO

Index

Unbound is the world's first crowdfunding publisher, established in 2011.

We believe that wonderful things can happen when you clear a path for people who share a passion. That's why we've built a platform that brings together readers and authors to crowdfund books they believe in – and give fresh ideas that don't fit the traditional mould the chance they deserve.

This book is in your hands because readers made it possible. Everyone who pledged their support is listed below. Join them by visiting unbound.com and supporting a book today.

Elizabeth Abbott
Russell Abbott
AbbottMoody Associates
   Ltd.
Oz Ablett
Chris Adams
Drew Adams
Keith Adsley
Luke Agbaimoni
Aisha
Brian Aitchison
Luke Alder
Nicholas Aleksander
Wes Alexander
Susan Algie
Lulu Allison
Graham Almond
Matt Alofs
Frances Ambler
Anita Amies
Mark Amies
Leigh Anderson
William Arnold
Mara Arts
Richard Ashcroft
Richard Aspden
Paul Austen
Ben Austwick
Karen Averby
Michelle Ayling
Antony Badsey-Ellis
Alison Bailey
Chris Bailey
Nicola Bailey
Aidan Oliver Baker

Christopher Baker
Danny Baker
Liz and Chris Baker
Tom Baker
John Band
Colin Bannard
Nicola Bannock
Neil Barker
Gordon Barnes
Helen Barnes
Tim Barnsley
Robbie Barry
David Barton
Jason Batt
David Bauckham
Adam Baylis-West
Julie Beadle
M Beaney
Timothy Beecroft
Andy Beevers
Jo Beggs
Arash Behrooz
Colin Beirne
Jonathan Bell
Nigel Bell
Graham Bennett
Phillip Bennett-Richards
Julian Benton
Bruno Bernardo
David Bertram
James Bettley
Sean Bicknell
Rhiannon Bigham
David Bimpson
James Binning

Tim Bird
Rachel Birrell
Richard Bishop
John Blake
R P Blows
David Bonney
Charles Boot
Will Bowers
Chris Bowes
John Boxall
Stephen Boyd Davis
Joe Brady
Matt Bramford
Andrew Brattle
Andy Brereton
Jo Bridger
Lindsey Brodie
Robert Brook
Martin Brookes
Andrew Brooks
Adrian Brown
Mathew Browne
Tim Bryars
Ron Bull
Chris Bullock
Pauline Burdon
Patrick Burke
Owen Burkett
Melanie Burrows
Anthony Burton
Rosemary Burton
Nick Bush
Andrea Butcher
Clare Butler
Philip Butler

Arthur Byng Nelson
Patrick Byrne
Ian Callaghan
Will Callaghan
Piers Calver
Chris Campion
Thomas Canning
Jessica Cargill Thompson
Helen Carpenter
Jonathan Carr
Maria Carradice
Daniel Carrol
Phil Carroll-O'Kane
Benjamin Carter
Barry Caruth
Leo Cassarani
Steve Cawser
Tracy Chabot
Karan Chadda
Gosbert Chagula
Colin Chalmers
Steph Chamberlain
Timothy Chan
Barbara Chandler
Ambrose Chapel
Mark Chapman
Theo Chapple
Gaby Charing
Harry Charrington
Stuart Chatterton
Colin Cheesman
Anne Cheng
Anne Chesmore
John Cheston
Chris Chinnery
Neil Cholerton
Liz Christie
Carl Clare
Simon Clark
Ed Clarke
Samuel Clarke
Rob Clayton
Jeff Cleminson
Dominic Clifton
Andrew Clubb
Michael Cmar
Michael Coates
Tom Cochrane
James Coleman
Owen Collins
Richard Coltman
Martin Conder
James Condliffe
Alina Congreve
David Constable

Dave Convery
Inna Cook
Jacob Cook
Paul Cook
Kim Cooper
Mark E Cooper
Dr Kevin Cordes
Rosie Corlett
Ellie Cornell
Hannah Cottle
Nigel Coutts
Robert Cox
Nathaniel Cramp
John Cratchley
John Crawford
Anthony Creagh
Adam Creen
Mike Crilly
Paul Croft
Roger Crouch
Israel Crowe
Dr Jeanie Cruickshank
Mary R. Crumpton
Jonny Cuba
Jules Curran
Steve Currie
Russell Curtis
Guy Cuthbertson
Richard Cuthbertson
Gary Cutlack
Kristleifur Daðason
Robert Dagg
Patrick Daintith
Chris Darke
Susan Darling
Wendy Darling
Rishi Dastidar
Ron Daughtry
Bryan Davey
Genista Davidson
Bryn Davies
Faye W Davies
Matt Davies
Maurice Davies
Sydney Davies
Andrew Davis
Kim Davis
Laura Davis
Tony Davis
George Davson
Amir Dawoodbhai
A E Day
Guy de Jonquières
Lianne de Mello
Eric de Regnaucourt

Stephen de Riel
Stephen de Saulles
David De Smet
Charles Delahaye
Martin Delamere
Graeme Dennard
Roland Denning
Ian Denton
Joel Denton
Caroline Derry
Alan Devine
Traceyanne Devine
John Dexter
Jonathan Dibb
Paul Dicken
Michael Dillon
Elizabeth Dobson
David Dodd
Les Dodd
Ian & Rebecca Dodsworth
Alastair Doggett
Maria Donde
Clare Dowse
James Draper
Paul Drinkwater
Cory Driscoll
Gill Duane
Joshua Dully
Tim Dunn
Daniel Durling
Nicola Dwornik
Joe Dwyer
Sue Dwyer
Geoffrey Eagland
Phil Eaton
Andrew Eberlin
Kim Eccleston
Angela Edward
Ed Elloway
Sue Elwood
Andrew Emmerson
Joe Espinosa
David Evans
Rhiannon Evans
Robert Evans
Susie Fairweather
Jake Falcon
Alison Faraday
William Farrell
Simon Fathers
Sandra Fawcett
Rebecca Fazzalari
Matthew Fearn
Tony Felgate
James Felix

Paul Fellerman
Simon Felton
Stuart Ferguson
Mark Field
Caroline Finch-Stanford
Alan Finney
Robert Fiske
Joe Flatman
Hazel Fleming
Kathleen Fleming
Michael J Flexer
Matthew Foreman
Andy Fowler
Andrew Fox
Johnny Fox
Conrad Fox Robinson
Philip Frame
Julian Francis-Lawton
Rue Franklin
Michelle Franks
James Fraser
Matthew Freedman
Debby Freeman
Christopher French
Alan Fricker
Matthew Frost
Shaun Fry
Sarah and Andy G
Martin Gamage
Rob Gammage
Deborah Garfen
Bruce Gaston
Ciaran Gavin
Mark Geary
Amro Gebreel
Matthew Gibbons
Kirsty Gibbs
David Gibson
Chris Gilbert
Sam Gilbert
Christopher Gildert
Bob Giles
Emilie Giles
Harpreet Gill
Joris Gillet
Thomas Gittings
Mikhail Glushenkov
Martin Godfrey
Oliver Golden
George Goodfellow
Charlotte Goodhart
Richard Gooding
David Goodman
Joshua Goodwin
Laura Gordon

Sophie Gordon
Jeremy Gostick
Sue Gould
Brent Graham
Annie Grant
Liam Grant
Nick Grant
John Graves
Wendy Gray
Robert Green
Joanne Greenway
Dominic Gregory
James Gregory-Monk
Simon Gribben
Neil Griffin
Tim Grimes
Oliver Grimshaw
John Grindrod
Ushma Gudka-Chik
Carl Gulland
Robert Gurd
Caroline Hadley
Almar Haflidason
William Haggard
Heather Hall
Tom Hall
Lisa Hallam
Peter Halliday
Rob Halloway
Roxana Halls
Ellen Halstead
Dr Sarah Halton
James Hancock
David Handford
Anders Hanson
Sylvain Haon
Tom Happold
Ron Hardie
Gillian Hardy
Rushabh Haria
Andrew Harris
Pete Harris
Raymond Harris
Chris Harry
Martin Hart
Peter Hart
Philip Hart
Tony Hart
Ben and Michele Harvey
Nick Haseltine
Mohammed Hassan
Jamie Hawkins
John Haworth
Rafy Hay
Yvette Haynes

Enno Hebbelmann
Kenneth Henderson
Philip Hendrick
Carsten Hermann
Chris Herriman
Beverly Hetherington
Nick Higham
Iain Hill
Robert Hill
Christopher Hilton
Richard Himan
Andrew Hingston
Karen Hinojosa
Peter Hirschmann
John A Hobson
Jon Hockley
Andrew Hodges
Paul Hodges
Jason Hollington
Tony Holmes
John Holt
Mr C Holtham
Tony Homersham
Jeremy Honer
Jonathan Hope
Yvonne Hope
Virginia Hope-Rossides
Matthew Hopkins
Johnny Horth
Christopher Horton
Neal Houghton
Dan Howard
John Howard
Lily Howard
Tom Howard
Henry Howarth
Jonathan Howarth
Boris Howell
Nick Hubble
Jim Hughes
Anna Hull
Guy Hulse
Bruce Humby
Russ Humphrey
Nik Hunt
David Hunter
Gabriel Huntley
Terry Hurley
Peter Hutton
Josh Ibrahim
Michael Imber
Steve Ingall
Phil Ivens
Greg Ivings
Charlie Jackson

Adam Jacob
David James
Anthony Jarvis
James Jefferies
Alice Jenks
Paul Jenner
Matthew Jennings
Trish Johns
Rosemary Johnsen
Colin Johnson
Caleb Johnstone-Cowan
Chris Jones
Howard Jones
John Jones
Matthew P Jones
Steve Jones
Amit Kamal
Giorgos Karatziolas
Eddie Kavanagh
John Kaye
Darron Keeling
Anthony Keen
Clive Kelly
Kate Kelly
Karen Kemal
Paul Kemp
Joseph Kennedy
Mohammad Khpal
Patrick Kidd
Dan Kieran
Jon Kingsbury
Che Knights
Andy Knott
James Knowling
Beaudry Kock
Joanne Koukis
Carina Krause
Bob Kraushaar
Anna Kristoffersen
Michael Kümmling
Pierre L'Allier
Harmohn Laehri
Darnell LaGuerre
Stephen Laing
Caitriona Lambe
Nickolas Lambrianou
Gary Lang
Emily Lang-Bell
Mike Lauff
Michael Law
John Law Baker
Richard Leach
Emma Leahy
Joseph Leake
Garth Leder

Michael Ledger-Lomas
Ian Lee
Nicholas Lee
Alexander Legg
Marianne Lester-George
Frederick Levy
Chris Lewis
Samantha Li-Fox
Scott Linder
David Link
Sophie Linwood
Robert Lipfriend
Tamasin Little
littlepurplegoth
Paul Robert Lloyd
Dan Lockton
Deborah Loe
Deborah Loftus
Con Logue
Basil Long
David Longmuir
William Lord
Simon Lowe
Nick Luff
Michael Luffingham
Paul Lunn
James Lusher
William Lusty
Naomi Luxford
Jane MacCuish
Alex Macgregor Mason
Jane Macintyre
Ian Macready
Drew Maftoc
Robi Maftoc
Jeremiah Mahadevan
Faiza Mahmood
Mark Maidment
Chris Mallaband
Sarra Manning
Steve Mannion
The Manser Practice
    Architects + Designers
Adrian Mansi
Anthony Maplesden
David March
Mohammed Marikar
Malte Markert
Krishna Maroo
Evelyn Marr
Kate Marsden
Greg Marsh
Hugh Martin
Ian Martin
Yant Martin-Keyte

Darren Maughan
Richard Mawle
Callum May
Elizabeth May
Alan Mayes
Richard Mayson
Andy McColl
Jon McCorkell
Hugh McEwen
Steve McGee
Chris McGill
Katy McGilvray
Ian McGraw
John McKay
Ben McKeown
Susan Ann Mclaren
Duane McLemore
Andrew McLintock
Ruth McManus
Emily McMinn
Albertina McNeill
Sian Meades-Williams
Paul Meads
Lee Melin
Mark Meredith
Di Middleton
H Mikhail
Luke Miller
Willie Miller
Samantha Milton
Nina-Sophia Miralles
Edward Mirzoeff
Joanne Mirzoeff
'Ley Missailidis
Holly Mitchell
Jake Mitchell
John Mitchinson
Andrew Moffatt
Neil Moorcroft
Blake Moore
Julie Moore
Tarmini Mootoosamy
Mark Morfett
Sarah Morris
Stephen Morris
Helen Mortell
Richard Moseley
Chris Moss
Graham Moss
Graham Murray
Sean Murray
Carlo Navato
Katrina Navickas
Kate Nelson
Mark Nesbitt

Pamela Newick
Ray Newman
David Newsome
Hazel Nicholson
Kevin Nicholson
Daniel Nixon
Kirsty Noble
David Nolan
Ashley Norris
Lukas Novotny
Peter Nowell
Conrad Nowikow
Matthew Nudds
Darren Nuttall
Des O'Donoghue
Mark O'Neill
Sean O'Neill
Sue Odell
Maaret Ojalehto
Mick Oldham
Gregory Olver
Richard Oosterom
Diana Oppe
Roland Orchard
Fiona Orsini
Caroline Osbourn
Tom Otteson
Gwyn Owen
Julia Owen
Lauriann Owens
Michael Paley
Sue Pallot
Ian Palmer
Andy Parrott
Graham Partridge
Michael Passingham
Michael Payne
Oliver Pearcey
Lynn Pearson
Noreen Pearson
Philip Pearson
Matthew Pencharz
Adam Pepper
Robyn Percy
Maria Teresa Perez
John Simon Perring
John Perry
Keith Perry
Will Pethen
Jane Petrie
Fei Phoon
Simon Pickford
Simon Pilkington
David Piper
Ruth Piper

Marco Pirroni
Jon Pitt
Ian Pleace
Adam Plotkin
Helena Poldervaart
Justin Pollard
Steve Pollard
Kirsty Pope
Martin Popplewell
Anne Porcheron
Steve Porter
Post Utility
Clare Price
Robert Priest
Patrick Pringle
Lois Pryce
Philip Pullman
Andrew Purdy
Nick Purser
Dr Quince
Ruby Quince
Stanley Quinnell
Mr R.Thos. Rainbow
Lesley Ramm
JP Rangaswami
Ol Rappaport
Daniel Rawling
Michael Rayment
Stephen Read
Simon Reap
Nicholas Redding
Bethan Rees
Louise Rees
Emma Renton
Mark Rich
Mark Richards
Will Richards
Jon Rickards
Barbara Rickwood
Geoff Rideout
Gareth Rimmer
Helen Rimmer
John Rivers
Anne Roache
Paul Robins
Jane Robinson
Sarah Anastasia Robinson
Tom Robson
Fred Rodgers
Steve Roffey
Glen Rollings
Donna Romano
Michael Rosen
Elliot Ross
Vanessa Ross

Diana Rossborough
Karina Rosu
Anna Route
David Rowlands
Liberty Rowley
Gavin Rowney
Ines Ruf
Daniel Ruff
Tjerk Ruimschotel
Ian Runacres
Eleanor Ruskin
Darren Russell
Edward Russell
Nicola Rutt
Sean Rutter
Deborah Ryan
Will S
Greg Sadler
Richard Salkeld
Judith Salomon
Puskas Salts
Vasily Samitin
Chris Sampson
Oliver Saunders
Jon Savage
Mark Savage
Jon Saville
Andy Savvides
Nicholas Scanlan
David Scheutz
Mark Scorah
David Scott
Lisa Scott
Simon Scott
Brian Screaton
Sheila Seacroft
Eiki Sekine
Joseph Seliga
John Seligmann
Monica Setrem
Madeleine Severin
Stephen Shahbazian
Liam Shanahan
Martyn Shaw
Andrew Shepherd
Phil Sheppard
Keith Sherratt
Matthew Shillaber
Lucy Shipton
Daniel Sidi
Maureen Simkins
Rossington Simmonds
Nick Simmons
Hazel Simpson
Cameron Sinclair-Fox